DOCTORS' LATIN

DOCTORS' LATIN

A Miscellany of Latin and Greek Phrases

Keith Souter

Fellow of the Royal College of
General Practitioners

ROBERT HALE · LONDON

ISBN-10: 0-7090-7950-8
ISBN-13: 978-0-7090-7950-7

Robert Hale Limited
Clerkenwell House
Clerkenwell Green
London EC1R 0HT

2 4 6 8 10 9 7 5 3 1

Typeset in 10/12pt Palatino
by e-type, Liverpool
Printed in Great Britain by St Edmundsbury Press Limited,
Bury St Edmunds, Suffolk
Bound by Woolnough Bookbinding Limited

Contents

In memory of my late father-in-law,
Revd Leslie Kitchen, MA.

Orsorum

'The First Few Words'

For a so-called 'dead' language Latin has always enjoyed a healthy association with the medical profession. Indeed, there is an impression that doctors consider themselves a bit superior to everyone else because the use of Latin makes them feel erudite and scholarly, and that it maintains the mystique of the healing profession.

It has to be admitted that there is an element of truth in all this. The fact is that Latin is the international language of medicine, just as it has been since the days of Ancient Rome. Although the Romans were never great innovators in the field of medicine, they translated the medical works of their neighbours, the Greeks, into Latin and then disseminated the texts across their empire. And in that they did as great a service to mankind as they did when they gave us the aqueduct, concrete and the Roman calendar.

About ninety to ninety-five per cent of all medical terms are based on Latin and Greek. Most of the anatomical terms and the scientific names of micro-organisms are of Latin origin, whereas many of the pathological and medical terms come from Greek, or a mixture of the two languages. The Greek terms reflect the knowledge and skills of the early Classical Greek physicians whereas the Latin terminology comes both from antiquity and from the Renaissance, when Latin became the language of science and medicine. The beauty of it is that because Latin is a dead language it is unchanging, hence its suitability as an international medical nomenclature.

When we use the word 'Latin' we actually use a generic word encompassing several types of Latin. Old Latin is the oldest recorded Latin, dating back as far as the sixth century. Classical Latin is the language of the educated people of Ancient Rome, the Latin of the great prose-writers, Livy, Tacitus and Cicero and of the great poets, Horace, Virgil and Ovid. Late Latin is the language of the Church, and New Latin is the type that most interests us here, since it is the Latin used since the Renaissance when medicine became a science.

This miscellany of doctors' Latin is designed to give the reader an insight into the language of doctors, from the multi-syllabic diagnostic labels and the complex anatomical terms to the indecipherable written language of prescriptions. Scattered throughout are the Latin mottos of the great medical institutions, the Latin axioms and maxims of generations of doctors, and opinions expressed about and by doctors from days gone by. It is worth pointing out, however, that purists may find that medical Latin does not always follow the rules of Classical Latin.

The entry for each term starts by giving its Latin origin (or, where appropriate, the Greek origin). This is followed by a brief outline of its usage, history or features of interest. So come, welcome to the world of Celsus, Cicero and Vesalius, and to the language of your current doctor.

Acknowledgements

Mark Twain once likened the writing of a book to the process of nursing a patient through a long illness. Visiting the study every day is like attending to the patient in the sickroom. Once the patient has recovered and is ready to be discharged the sickroom can be made up again. You get rid of all the reminders of the process and spring-clean the room. And as you do that, as you begin to clear away the dusty reference books, file the sheets of paper with scrawled jottings and generally bring order to chaos, you realize what friends you have become with all those bits and pieces that go to make up a book. And that is when you have to say 'thank you'.

It is quite impossible to write a book on doctor's Latin without expressing gratitude to those people who first wrote in Latin. I therefore thank the great poets, Horace, Ovid and Virgil, the great prose-writers, Livy, Pliny, Tacitus and Cicero, and all of those early writers on medicine, whether they were non-doctors like Celsus, or highly qualified physicians like William Harvey, who used the scientific language of Latin to deliver their work to posterity. And then I thank all of the anatomists of the past who meticulously named each and every muscle, artery, vein and nerve of the body to make life difficult for generations of medical students, myself included.

The texts that I had to revisit to produce this little miscellany are almost too numerous to mention, yet there are a few that have to be singled out: *Gray's Anatomy*, *Grant's Method of Anatomy*, *Bigger's Handbook of Bacteriology*, *Black's Medical Dictionary*, W. Gurney Benham's *Book of Quotations*. All of them have been put back on the shelves. The more modern texts like William Casselman's *Dictionary of Medical Derivations*, Tore Janson's *A Natural History of Latin*, and Eugene Ehrlich's *A Dictionary of Latin Tags and Phrases* have all now been moved from their regular space beside the computer, and I miss them already. And, of course, I must thank the myriad of authors who have made their works available on the Internet.

Altogether it has been an enjoyable trip for me, as it has taken me back to my anatomy days, my pathology books and my old case notes. My researches have introduced me to the great writers of the past, whose words of wisdom, wit and sagacity still live on in some of the axioms, maxims and phrases that I have had the pleasure of unearthing for this book.

Apologia

This book is intended as a work of entertainment, rather than a textbook of medical Latin. I, the author, am a simple medical practitioner rather than a linguist or a Latin scholar. The derivations given are as accurate as I can ascertain, so any mistakes are mine and I apologize if any scholar is offended by my lack of expertise. Remember, *humanum est errare*.

Dr Keith Souter

Doctors' Latin

A

Abdomen

The cavity that hides the entrails – from *abdere*, 'to hide' and *omentum*, 'entrails'. The name for the anatomical cavity between the thorax (chest) and pelvis. Its contents include the liver, spleen, kidneys, pancreas, stomach, and small and large intestines. The term was first used by Pliny in AD 50. Whereas most people pronounce the word *ab*domen, doctors use a solemn tone of voice and say ab*do*men. Cynics have suggested that it is due to a belief among the medical profession that they think they know more than anyone else about the word. In actual fact, stressing the second syllable is the correct way to pronounce this word because the stress should be placed on the second or third syllable from the end in Latin. In other words, it seems that doctors probably do know more about the abdomen than everybody else – which is just as well really.

Abducens

The eye muscle that 'leads away from (the midline)' – from *ab*, 'away' and *ducens*, 'leading'. The *abducens* is the name for the *lateral rectus* muscle of the eye. It is one of six muscles that are attached to each eyeball and which move it in different directions. The *lateral rectus* and the *medial rectus* muscles move the eyeball from side to side.

Abducent nerve

The nerve that operates outwards movement of the eyeball through its action on the *lateral rectus*, or abducens muscle. The abducent nerve is the sixth cranial nerve. It operates the abducens muscle to make the eyeball look outwards. It is a very delicate nerve with a relatively long pathway, which puts it at risk of damage or nervous system disease, which could produce a squint. See *abductor*.

Abductor

A muscle that moves a part away from the midline – from *ab*, 'away', and *ducere*, 'to draw or lead'. Most of the joints have abductor muscles attached to them, which move them outwards. Many of these muscles have multiple actions, and the following have specific abduction action:

Abductor digiti minimi – the abductor muscle of the fifth digit (little finger or little toe). It moves the little finger or little toe outwards.

Abductor hallucis – the abductor muscle of the big toe, from *hallux*, 'great toe'.

Abductor pollicis brevis – the short muscle of the thumb, from *pollex*, 'thumb', and *brevis*, 'short'. It moves the thumb at right angles to the palm of the hand. An extremely important muscle which is partly responsible for us having opposable thumbs. This ability allowed our evolutionary ancestors to grasp branches and later on to fashion and operate tools.

Abductor pollicis longus – the long muscle of the thumb, from *pollex*, 'thumb', and *longus*, long. This muscle arises in the mid-forearm and is inserted into the thumb. It helps to flex the wrist and to abduct the thumb. The 'thumbs up' muscle.

Ab imo pectore
'From the heart' – from the bottom of the heart, or the bottom of the chest, meaning to speak sincerely. This expression is attributed to Julius Caesar.

Ab incunabulis
From the cradle, from childhood. The responsibility of a physician is said to start from the cradle.

Ablactation
The process of weaning a baby off milk on to solid foods – from *ab*, 'away', and *lactens*, 'sucking milk'.

Ablation
The removal of a part of the body, usually by surgery – from *ablatum*, 'to carry away'. Originally the word meant removal of a disease or illness by some medical means but by the nineteenth century it came to be specifically associated with surgical removal of an organ, limb or tissue. Nowadays it may refer to surgical removal or to removal or suppression of tissue by the non-surgical use of lasers or microwaves.

Ablutophobia
Fear of washing or bathing – from the Latin *ablutio*, from *abluere*, 'to wash', and the Greek *phobos*, 'fear'.

Abortion
Miscarriage – from *ab*, 'away', and *oriri*, 'appear, be born, arise'. A spontaneous abortion is a natural miscarriage, as

opposed to a therapeutic abortion or termination of pregnancy.

Abrasion
A graze – from *ab*, 'away' and *rasionis*, 'scraping'.

Abscess
A collection of pus – from *ab*, 'away', and *cessus*, 'thrown'. Abscesses occur when an area of tissue becomes infected and the body walls off the infection to keep it from spreading. The original concept was that pus formation represented the body's attempt to throw out disease. Pus is an accumulate of fluid, living and dead white blood cells, dead tissue, and bacteria or other foreign invaders or materials. Abscesses can form in almost every part of the body and may be caused by infectious organisms, parasites, and foreign materials. See *pus, ubi pus, ibi evacua*.

Absente febri
'In the absence of fever.' The abbreviation *abs. feb* used to be written in prescriptions when it was intended that a particular remedy should be given provided that a fever was not present.

Accessory
An organ or tissue that seems to have been added to the main organ or tissue – from *accedere*, 'to be added to'. These are often congenital anomalies that are not necessarily of any significance. Thus one can have an accessory or additional lobe of the liver, lung or kidney. Sometimes, however, an accessory tissue can cause problems, as in the Wolff-Parkinson-White syndrome, in which an accessory electrical conducting tissue in the

heart results in the individual experiencing frequent palpitations. Non-surgical ablation (see above) of the tissue usually brings about a cure.

The *accessory nerve* is the eleventh cranial nerve. It is considered to be functionally accessory to the vagus nerve, which is the tenth cranial nerve. This nerve operates the muscles that allow you to shrug your shoulders. It assists the vagus nerve in operating the pharynx and larynx.

Acetabulum
Hip socket – literally, vinegar cup or cruet, from *acetum*, 'vinegar', and *bulum*, meaning 'container'. Pliny the Elder wrote about the similarity between the hip socket and a vinegar cruet. It is the socket in the pelvis into which the femur or thigh bone fits like a ball into a socket. See *femur*.

Achillea millefolium
'Yarrow.' This herb has many country names, including salve of Achilles, soldier's woundwort, staunchweed, and sanguinary. Legend had it that Achilles used yarrow poultices to staunch the wounds of his soldiers. It is used in herbal medicine and in homoeopathic medicine as the remedy Millefolium. An active ingredient, the alkaloid achilleine, has been found to reduce bleeding.

Achilles tendon
See *tendo calcaneus*.

Acid
Sour tasting – from *acidus*, 'sour', or 'acid'. There are many acids produced by and used in the metabolic processes of the body. For example, amino acids, citric acid, fatty acids,

folic acid, hydrochloric acid, and the nucleic acids – deoxyribonucleic acid (DNA) and ribonucleic acid (RNA).

Acidosis

A state of excess acid – from *acidus*, 'sour' or 'acid', and *-osis*, which is used to indicate a state of disorder. The body has to maintain a balance between its acids and its bases (alkalis) by various metabolic processes carried out by the blood, kidneys and lungs. A state of acidosis can occur in diabetes mellitus, starvation, severe dehydration, prolonged diarrhoea and in severe emphysema.

Aconitum napellus

This herb, known as monkshood, friar's cap or auld wife's huid, contains the poison aconite. It has wide use in homoeopathic medicine as an acute remedy in shock and trauma.

Acoustic

Hearing – from the Greek *akoustikos*, 'pertaining to hearing', from *akouein*, 'to hear'. The *acoustic nerve* (also called the *auditory* or the *vestibulocochlear nerve*) is the eighth cranial nerve, which supplies the *cochlea* (the organ of hearing) and the *vestibule* and semicircular canals (the balance organs) in the inner ear.
See *cochlea* and *vestibule*.

Acrophobia

Fear of heights – from the Greek words *akros*, meaning 'high', and *phobos*, 'fear'.

Acupuncture

Method of treatment by the use of needles – from *acus*, 'sharp' and *punctum*, 'a prick'. Acupuncture is the name given to the system of medicine that was developed in China, reputedly in about 4000 BCE. It is a method of treatment that has become increasingly accepted by Western orthodox medicine.

Acute
Sharp, or of rapid onset – from *acutus*, meaning 'sharp', or 'pointed'.
In medicine an acute illness is of quick onset.

Ad
'Up to.' The preposition *ad* used to be written in prescription when a limit was being placed on a number of doses, so no more than that number would be given.

Addendus
'To be added.' In prescription-writing, the abbreviation *add.* could be used when something is to be added – to water, for example.

Ad duas vices
'For two times.' In prescription-writing the abbreviation *ad 2 vic.* would be used when something was to be done only two times.

Adductor muscles
Muscles that 'move a part towards' the midline of the body. There are three adductor muscles in the thigh: *adductor brevis*, the short adductor muscle of the lower leg, *adductor longus* – the long adductor muscle of the lower leg, and *adductor magnus* – the big adductor muscle of the lower leg. These muscles are commonly strained in kickers and this is often referred to as a groin injury.

Adductor hallucis – one of the muscles that move the big toe inwards. From *ad*, 'towards', and *ducere*, 'to lead', 'to draw', and *hallux*, 'big toe'.

Adductor pollicis – the short adductor muscle of the thumb, from *pollex*, thumb. It draws the thumb across the palm.

ad finem
'At or near to the end.' Essentially, in the terminal stages of an illness, or close to death. Cf. *in extremis*.

Adipose
Fat tissue – from the Latin *adipis*, 'fat', and *osus*, meaning 'full of'. In medicine, adipose tissue is the name for the layer of fat-filled cells under the skin and around many of the internal organs. Surprisingly, the only organ that does not have an adipose layer is the brain, making the derogatory term 'fathead' a rather silly remark.

Adipocere
'Waxy fat', also known as grave fat! This is the name given to a soapy greyish-white coloured substance that forms on a dead body under conditions of high humidity and high environmental heat. It consists principally of insoluble salts of fatty acids, such as oleic, palmitic and stearic acids.

Ad libitum
'Take freely, as necessary.' In writing a prescription, the abbreviation *ad lib.* may be used. Generally, this would only be used with an innocuous remedy that does not contain a drug, such as a simple cough linctus, because there would be no danger of producing a drug intoxication. See *pro re nata*.

Admove
'Apply (thou).' In prescription-writing the abbreviation *admov.* could be used as an indication to the chemist to instruct the patient to apply some cream, ointment or embrocation to himself or herself.

Ad nauseam
'To the point of sickness.' Essentially meaning to go on and on.

Ad partem affectum
'To the part affected.' A prescription might say that an ointment, cream or salve should be applied *ad. part affect*, meaning to the affected part.

Adrenal
The gland that sits upon the kidney – from *ad*, 'up to', and *renalis*, 'of the kidney'. There is an adrenal gland above each kidney. It produces many hormones, including adrenaline, the 'fight or flight hormone' that makes you feel excited or fearful.

Ad sanitatem gradus est novisse morbum
'It is a step towards health to know what the complaint is.'

Adstante febri
'While the fever lasts.' In prescription-writing, the abbreviation *ads. feb.* could be used to indicate that a remedy or procedure should be continued as long as a fever persists.

Ad tertiam vicem
'For three times.' In prescription-writing the abbreviation *ad 3 vic.* would be used when something was to be done only three times.

Aegrescitque medendo
'He becomes more ill through remedies' – Virgil, the *Aeneid*, 12, 46. See *Virgil*.

Aegri somni
'A sick man's dreams', or 'troubled dreams'. Horace's writings suggest that they are the same as our modern idea of hallucinations.

Aegrotat
'He is sick' – from *aegrotare*, 'to be sick'. Essentially, this means a note from the doctor. It also refers to a degree that is conferred upon a candidate who was too ill to finish the course or to take the final examination.

Aegroto dum anima est, spes est
'As long as a sick person is conscious, there is still hope.'

Aetiology
'The causation' – from the Greek *aitia*, 'cause', and *logos*, 'study of'. In medicine it is important to consider the aetiological factors in an illness, the factors that are likely to have contributed to or directly caused an illness.

Agita
'Shake.' In writing a prescription the abbreviation *agit* may be used, meaning to shake before taking. This is for suspensions or emulsions, to ensure mixing of the preparation.

Agoraphobia
'Fear of open spaces' – from the Greek *agora*, 'market place', and *phobos*, 'fear of'. People subject to this condi-

tion may feel unable to leave their own house. It can be incredibly debilitating.

Alma mater
'Kind mother.' This is used to refer to one's old school, college, university or medical school.

Alopecia
'Hair loss' – from *alopecia*, 'a fox with mange'. Originally this referred to the appearance of a fox with mange, with resultant patchy loss of fur. There are variants:

Alopecia Areata – the most commonly used term, which covers all forms of the disease.

Alopecia areata barbae – the term for an *alopecia areata* lesion found in the region of the beard hair.

Alopecia areata ophiasis – the term used for an *alopecia areata* lesion limited to extension along the scalp margin. *Ophiasis* comes from the Greek for snake, due to the winding, snaking pattern the hair loss has over the back of the head. The term was originally used by Celsus in AD 30.

Alopecia partialis – the name given to specify patchy hair loss.

Alopecia totalis – the name given to specify *alopecia areata*, where all scalp hair is lost, but other body hair remains.

Alopecia universalis – the name given to specify alopecia areata where all scalp and body hair is lost.

Alternis diebus

'Every other day.' In prescription-writing the abbreviation *alt. die* could be written to mean that something had to be taken or done on alternate days.

Alternis horis

'Every other hour.' In prescription-writing the abbreviation *alt. hor.* or *AH*, could be used to indicate that something had to be taken or done on alternate hours.

Alveolus and alveoli

'Hollows' – from *alveus*, 'trough or small hollows'. There are two types of alveolus (plural alveoli) – dental alveoli or tooth sockets and lung alveoli, or the little air sacs at the end of the airways.

Ambulance

'A vehicle that carries patients' – from *ambulantia*, 'the act of walking'.

Ambulatory

'While walking' – from *ambulare*, 'to walk'. Ambulatory testing of the heart or the blood pressure is often done while the patient goes about his or her daily activities, a recording apparatus being worn all the time.

Amnesia

'Loss of memory' – from the Greek *amnesia*, meaning 'forgetfulness'. Amnesia, although beloved by Hollywood and television scriptwriters, is an alarming and often frightening state in which memory is disturbed or even lost. It can be caused by trauma, disease and certain drugs, when the way in which the brain works may be impaired. These are called organic causes. Alternatively, it can be caused by functional or unconscious psychological defence mechanisms, when some event, situation or experience is so disturbing to the mind that the memory of it is suppressed. This may result in other memories being lost as well. Anterograde amnesia refers to memory loss for new or recent events, as opposed to retrograde amnesia in which past events are forgotten. *Lacunar amnesia* is where a specific thing is forgotten; *traumatic amnesia* follows a head injury and usually relates to the traumatic event itself; *hysterical amnesia* occurs after a huge psychological trauma, producing the classic Hollywood wanderer with no memory.

Ampulla
'A saccular pouch' – from the Latin *ampulla*, meaning 'jug'. There are several ampullas described in anatomy: in the ear, the seminal ducts, the uterus and the rectum.

Anaemia
'A reduced concentration of red blood cells' – from the Greek *an*, 'without' or 'not', and *haima*, 'blood'. There are many causes of anaemia, including haemorrhage, deficiency of iron, folic acid, vitamin B_{12}.

Anaesthesia
'Reduction in sensation', often by inducing unconsciousness – from the Greek *anaesthesia*, meaning 'insensibility'. In pre-anaesthetic days surgery was a brutal affair, often depending upon the use of alcohol to produce insensibility. The science of anaesthetics has allowed the most amazing surgical procedures to become commonplace.

Analgesia
'Freedom from pain' – from the Greek *an*, 'without', and *algesia*, 'pain'. All sorts of herbs and drugs have an analgesic or painkilling effect.

Anatomy
The study of the human body in all its internal and external details. Traditionally this has been done by dissection. The name comes from the Greek *ana*, 'up', and the Greek *tome*, 'a cutting or a slicing'. It literally means 'cutting up', indicating that the true study can only be done by actual dissection of the organs and tissues. Although the Ancient Egyptians developed some knowledge of anatomy through their practice of mummification of the dead, they did not apply this knowledge as fully as they might have done in their practice of medicine. The Greek doctor, Galen, began a scientific study of anatomy through the dissection of animals. His work formed the basis of the subject until the fourteenth and fifteenth centuries, when dissection of a limited number of cadavers was permitted in the medical schools. Leonardo da Vinci undertook quite extensive studies as a private individual but his work was not really made available to the medical community. It fell to the likes of Andreas Vesalius (1514–64), Bartolomeo Eustachi (1513–74), William Harvey (1514–64) and John Hunter (1728–93) to push back the frontiers and develop the subject into a true science, the foundation of modern medicine. See *Eustachi, Galen, Harvey, Hunter* and *Vesalius*.

Anatomy of Melancholia
In 1621, Robert Burton, an Oxford don, published *The Anatomy of Melancholy*, a six-volume work, which was essentially the first major textbook on the subject of

depression. It covered the subject from the viewpoints of astrology, medicine, philosophy and proto-psychology. In it he produced a model of consciousness, which, although flawed, gave a framework with which people could work. Its influence continued for at least two centuries. It remains a fascinating classic of renaissance literature.

Angina pectoris
Severe (heart) chest pain – from *angina*, 'choking pain', and *pectoris*, 'chest'. Angina pectoris is the crushing chest pain that results from lack of oxygen to the heart. It is usually relieved by rest or by taking a spray of a nitrate solution under the tongue.

Anorexia nervosa
Literally, 'nervous lack of appetite in women' – from the Greek *an*, 'without', and *orexis*, 'appetite' or 'eating', and *nervosa*, the feminine of *nervosus*, 'nervous'. This condition was known in antiquity, although we think of it as a modern phenomenon. It belongs to the group of conditions that we call *dysmorphophobias*, or body image problems (from the Greek words *dys*, 'bad' or 'difficult', *morphe*, 'form or shape' and *phobos*, 'fear'). It is a complex and still poorly understood psycho-physiological disorder, usually occurring in young women, which is character- ized by an abnormal fear of becoming obese, a distorted self-image, a persistent unwillingness to eat, and severe weight loss. It is often accompanied by self-induced vomiting, excessive exercise, malnutrition, amenorrhea, and other physiological changes. See *bulimia.*

Ante
'Before.'

Ante cibos
'Take before food.' In writing a prescription, the abbreviation *a.c.* is used when it is important that a medicine be taken on an empty stomach in order to enhance its absorption.

Ante meridiem
'Take before noon.'

Antenatal
'Before birth.'

Anterior
'More in front.'

Anti-
'Against' – a Greek prefix.
Not to be confused with *ante*, the Latin word meaning 'before'.

Antibiotic
A drug that works literally against life – from the Greek *biotikos*, 'life'. Antibiotics are active against many bacterial micro-organisms, but not at all against viruses or fungi. There are several groups of antibiotics, including the penicillins. In orthodox Western medicine there are many 'anti' drugs: antidepressants, anticonvulsants, antidiarrhoeals, and so forth.

Antidote
A drug that works against something, generally a poison – from the New Latin *antidotum*, 'given to act against'. Thus an antidote would be given against a snake venom, for example.

Antipyretic
A medicine that lowers a fever – from Greek *anti* and *pyretos*, 'fever'. This word has superseded the old word 'febrifuge'. See *febrifuge*.

Antiseptic
'Against sepsis' – from Greek *anti* and *sepsis*, 'rotting'. An antiseptic is, therefore, something that prevents or works against a rotting condition or an infection.

Anus
The last orifice of the bowel – from *anus*, 'a ring'. This relates to the circular muscle at the back passage. There are two anal sphincters, one internal and one external, which open and close it. See *Sphincter*.

Aorta
The great blood vessel that carries blood from the heart – from the Greek word *aorte*, coined by the great Aristotle himself!

Aphrodisiac
A drug that enhances sexual desire – from the Greek *aphrodisiakos*, meaning 'sexual pleasure'. This word is itself derived from the Greek goddess of love, Aphrodite.

Apoplexy
'A stroke' – from the Greek *apo*, 'down', and *plexia*, 'a striking' – literally 'a striking down'. It is an archaic term, rarely used.

Apothecary
Someone who prepares and dispenses drugs – from the Greek *apo*, 'down', and *theca*, 'store', and the Latin *arius*,

'one who works'. The *apotheca* was originally a place where wines, spices and herbs were stored. During the thirteenth century the name apothecary became associated with someone who ran such a storehouse or shop. Interestingly, they belonged to the Guild of Pepperers, which had been formed in 1180. They were subsequently joined by the spicers (who spiced wine). The pepperers eventually broke off and became grocers, while the apothecaries continued spicing wines and developed skills in pharmacy. By the early seventeenth century they had effectively become community pharmacists and, in 1627, the Worshipful Society of Apothecaries of London was granted a royal charter. Since 1815 the society has been able to license candidates to practise medicine. Prospective apothecaries were taken on as apprentices and allowed, after a period of several years, to take examinations that would permit them to gain a licence to practise medicine. The Worshipful Society of Apothecaries is still involved in licensing doctors as part of the United Examining Board. See *opifer que per orbem dicor*.

Appendicectomy
The surgical removal of the appendix – from *appendix* and the Greek – *-ectome*, 'removal of'.

Appendix
The small blind ending of bowel arising from the caecum in the right lower part of the abdomen – from the Latin words *ad*, which by elision became *ap*, and *pendix*, 'hanging part'.

Aqua
'Water.'

Aqua menthae piperitae

'Peppermint water.' Peppermint water and several other types of 'water' were formerly routinely used in making up medicines. They were sometimes used, as in this case, as carminatives, or to simply make the unpalatable more palatable.

Aqua vitae

'Water of life.' The old alchemists used various distilled spirits to prolong life. They termed them *aqua vitae* or the elixir of life. The Scots also claim 'the water of life' as their own, in the Gaelic *uisge beatha*, translated into English as 'whisky.'

Aquosus languor

'Dropsy', or 'the watery weakness' – from *aqua*, 'water', and *languere*, 'to be faint'. See *digitalis purpurea* and *hydrops*.

Areola

The pigmented area around the nipple – from *area*, 'open space', and *ola* meaning 'small'; essentially 'the court-yard around the nipple'.

Ars longa, vita brevis

'The art is long, life is short.' This is an abbreviated Latin translation of the first aphorism of Hippocrates. The Art referred to is the craft of medicine, which takes a lifetime to learn. The full aphorism is: 'Life is short, and art long; the crisis fleeting; experience perilous, and decision diffi-cult.' See *Hippocrates of Cos*

Artery

A blood vessel that carries oxygenated blood from the heart to the tissues – from the Greek *aerterion*, meaning 'air-carrier'. This word originates from the days of the Ancient Greeks. The early anatomists thought that the arteries carried air, not blood. The reason they assumed this was because the arteries collapse and empty after death, most of the blood being found in the veins. But in fact the arteries carry oxygenated blood to the tissues, while the veins carry de-oxygenated blood back to the heart.

Ascaris lumbricoides

Literally, 'the long roundworm of the intestine' – from the Greek *ascarides*, 'gut worm', resembling the earthworm, *lumbroides*. This is the causative organism of the disease ascariasis, the commonest parasitic helminth disease in the world. It is rarely encountered in the developed world but is extremely common in the tropics. The worms can reach up to a foot in length.

Asclepius

Asclepius was the mythical Ancient Greek god of healing and a famous physician (known to the Romans as Aesculapius). His parents were the god Apollo and Coronis, a princess of Thessaly who died while Asclepius was still a child. Apollo entrusted the child's education to Chiron, a centaur who was famous for his knowledge of medicine, music and prophesy. Asclepius was an adept student and became so skilled in surgery and the use of medicinal plants that he could even restore the dead to life. This, of course, was considered the province of the gods alone, so Hades, the ruler of the dead complained to Zeus, ruler of all the gods, who killed Asclepius with a thunderbolt. Later, he was deified and joined the other gods on Mount Olympus. (The Greek gods seemed to be a forgiving bunch.) Asclepius had two daughters, Panacea and Hygeia who were also considered goddesses of health. See *Caduceus*.

Aspirin

Aspirin is one of the great medical stories of the modern age. At one time thought of as a medical joke, it has proved to be one of our most powerful and useful medicines. The actual drug acetylsalicylic acid (ASA) was first extracted from the plant meadowsweet (*Spiraea ulmaria*) in 1835. In 1897 Felix Hoffman, a German chemist synthesized ASA from a chemical similar to one found in willow bark. The name 'aspirin' was coined from '*A*' for acetylsalicylic acid, '*spir*' for *Spiraea ulmaria* and '*in*' because it gave the drug a scientific sounding name.

Atlas

The name given to the first cervical vertebra. It is so named after the Greek god who supported the weight of the world on his shoulders. It articulates with the second cervical vertebra, the axis, via the odontoid process or peg, which permits the atlas to rotate, so that the head can turn.

Atrium

Plural *atria* – the two upper chambers of the heart. From the Latin for the entrance hall, where visitors were greeted.

Aurea mediocritas

'The golden mean', hence 'Moderation in all things' – Horace, *Odes*. See *Horace*.

Auris dextra

Right ear. In writing a prescription, the abbreviation *a.d.* is used, to indicate that an ointment or drops are to be applied to the right ear.

Auris externa
'The outer ear.' This consists of the pinna or the visible ear. It collects sound waves and transmits them along the ear canal to the ear drum. See *otitis externa*.

Auris interna
'The internal ear.' This consists of the innermost part of the ear, containing the semicircular canals, vestibule and cochlea, the organs of balance and of hearing.
See *labyrinth*.

Auris media
'The middle ear.' This consists of the middle-ear chamber, which contains the ossicles. These transmit sound waves from the ear drum through to the organ of hearing. See *ossicles, otitis media*.

Auris sinistra
'Left ear.' In writing a prescription, the abbreviation *a.s.* is used, to indicate that an ointment or drops are to be applied to the left ear.

Auristillae
'The ear drops.' In prescription-writing the abbreviation *auristill.* could be used to indicate that ear drops were to be dispensed.

Aurus ultrae
'Apply to both ears.' In writing a prescription, the abbreviation *a.u.* is used, to indicate that an ointment or drops are to be applied to both ears.

Autopsy
Nowadays this equates with a post-mortem examina-

tion, or examination of the body after death. Originally, it had a different meaning. In the third century BCE, *autopsia* meant the observations that a physician made of his patient, as opposed to the information, *historia*, that the patient supplied.

Avicenna
Ibn Sina, or, in Persian, Abu Ali Husain ebn-e Abdollah ebn-e Sina (AD 980–1037) was a Persian physician, philosopher, and scientist. He was the author of 450 books, many of which were about philosophy and medicine. His most famous works are *The Book of Healing* and *The Canon of Medicine*, also known as the *Qanun*. His Latinized name is a corruption of *Ibn Sina*, the abbreviated version of his name by which he was known in Persia.

Axilla
'The armpit.'

Axis
The second cervical vertebra – from *axis*, 'an axle'. This vertebra articulates with the first cervical vertebra, the atlas, via the odontoid peg or process, thereby allowing the head to rotate. See *odontoid process*.

B

Bacillus

Rod shaped bacterium – from *bacillum*, 'little stick', or 'rod'. A bacillus is the name given to any rodlike bacterium, but it is also the name of a genus of bacteria found in the soil and dirt, such as *Bacillus anthracis*, which cause anthrax.

Bacon, Francis

Francis Bacon, first Viscount St Albans (1561–1626) was an English philosopher, statesman, spy, freemason and essayist. He was knighted in 1603, created Baron Verulam in 1618, and then Viscount St Albans in 1621. He started as a lawyer, but is famous as a key thinker in the scientific and philosophical revolution. In the *Baconian method*, which he pioneered, he aimed to test hypotheses by experiment and observation. He was a scientist generations ahead of his time. His death is attributed to his scientific zeal. In March 1626, while driving in the snow near Highgate, he decided to see whether low temperatures could preserve food. Accordingly he bought a fowl and stuffed it with snow. Unfortunately, while doing this he developed a cold, which subsequently developed into a fatal chest infection from which he died on 9 April 1626. See *scientia potestas est*.

Bacteria

Small rod or cane shaped micro-organisms – from the Greek *baktron*, 'rod' or 'cane', and *ion*, 'small'. Bacteria are micro-organisms that exist in the air, water and soil. Some produce disease and cause infections. Many others live on and in our bodies in a harmonious manner with us. When they cause infections, inflammation and pus formation are common results. They may be treated with antibiotics. See *antibiotics, pus* and *ubi pus, ibi evacua*. Most living things are classified by two names, a generic name and a specific name, according to a classification first worked out by Linnaeus. For example, *Escherichia coli*, a bowel bacterium and *Streptococcus viridans*, a bacterium often found in the mouth. See *Linnaeus*. The shapes of bacteria cells give clues to their identities. There are three main shapes: round (cocci), rods (bacilli) and spirals. See *bacillus, Staphylococcus, Streptococcus, Vibrio cholerae*.

Bacteriology
'The study of bacteria' – from the Greek *baktron* and *logos*, 'the study of something'. This is one of the main laboratory branches of medicine. Bacteriology is the study of bacteria, but in fact this is only a part of the whole subject of microbiology.

Bene diagnoscitur, bene curator
'Something that is well diagnosed can be cured well.'

Benign
'Favourable' – from *benignus*, 'mild'. In pathology a benign condition has a favourable outlook and is not cancerous. Cf. *malignant*.

Bi
Two, or two times – from *bis*, meaning 'twice', 'double'. This word is very important in medicine and is frequently used as a prefix, to refer to something having

two parts, or two sides. Hence the kidneys are bilateral, in that there is one on each side of the body. Spectacles may be bifocal, in that they have two sets of lenses, and something which is bipolar has two poles.

Bibe
'Drink.' In prescription-writing the abbreviation *bib* could be used to indicate that a particular water or tonic should be drunk, or taken so many times.

Biceps brachii
The muscle of the arm with two heads – from *bi*, 'two', and *cep*, derived from *caput*, 'head' and *bracchium* (singular) 'arm'. The bulging muscle that flexes the arm. It has two upper heads and a lower insertion at the elbow.

Biceps femoris
The two-headed muscles of the thigh – from *bi*, 'two', and *cep*, derived from *caput*, and *femoris*, derived from *femur*, 'the thigh'. One of the three hamstring muscles, together with *semitendinosus* and *semimembranosus*. These muscles help to straighten the leg at the hip and bend the leg at the knee. Understandably, runners and athletes often pull (strain) them. See *semitendinosus* and *semimembranosus*.

Bis in die
'Take twice daily.' In prescription-writing the abbreviation *b.i.d.* is usually used to mean take twice daily. Alternately, *bis die* also means twice daily with the abbreviation *b.d.*

Bis terve in die
'Two or three times a day.' In prescription-writing the abbreviation *b.t.i.d.* could be used to indicate that some-

thing should be taken two or three times a day, it being for the patients' discretion as to whether they need the third dose to control a symptom.

Bolus
A single shot of some medication – from the Geek *bole*, 'a throw'. In writing a prescription, the abbreviation *bol.* is used to indicate that a single dose is to be given, be that a pill or injection (which would also be specified).

Bona diagnosis, bona curatio
'Good diagnosis, good cure.'

Bona valetudo melior est quam maximae divitiae
'Good health is worth more than the greatest wealth.'

Bowel
Guts – actually, like little sausages – from *botellus*, meaning 'little sausage'. Surprisingly, this word derives from the days of the Roman centurion, when atrocious abdominal wounds could be seen, with the intestines splaying out like strings of sausages.

Brachial plexus
The main network of nerves that supply the upper limb – from *brachialis*, 'of the arm', and *plexus*, 'braid'. See *plexus*.

Bruxism
Teeth grinding – from the Greek word *brychein*, 'to gnash teeth'. This is a relatively common cause of chronic headaches, although the diagnosis is not always clear.

Bubo
Large infected lymph gland.

Bubonic plague

One of the horrific great plagues of the past, also known as the Black Death. The disease mainly affected rodents, but was passed to humans through the intermediate host, the flea. It was characterized by painful large glands or buboes, fever and by great red spots that turned black, hence the name. It swept through Europe from China in the early fourteenth century. The writer Boccaccio, of *Decameron* fame, said that it spread so fast that victims 'ate lunch with their friends and dinner with their ancestors in paradise.'

Bucca

Cheek – from *bucca*, meaning 'cheek'.

Buccinator

The trumpeter's muscle – from *buccina*, meaning 'trumpet'. The trumpets of Rome sounded out because of this muscle. It is a flat muscle that forms the main part of the cheek. It helps in chewing food by pressing the cheeks against the teeth, so that food will be manipulated between the teeth. Dogs do not have buccinators, so cannot chew in the same way that humans do. Dogs rip food into chunks and swallow them down, whereas the buccinator muscles allow us to grind food into a pulp, which is easier to swallow. Trumpeters, have to work their buccinators, as is obvious whenever you watch one at work. The buccinator is lined with a mucous membrane, the buccal membrane. It is from this membrane that cells can be removed in a buccal smear in order to determine sex of an individual (eg, in sports medicine to ensure that competitors are of the correct sex) and to obtain cells for DNA and chromosome testing for several genetic disorders. To feel your own buccinator in action pop your left index finger well into the right side of your cheek and perform chewing, sucking or blowing movements. If you don't feel your buccinator muscle compressing your finger, you would be wasting time ordering a new trumpet.

Bulbus oculi
'The eyeball.'

Bulimia
An eating disorder characterized by binge eating – from the Greek *bous*, meaning 'ox', and *limia*, hunger. This is not just a modern-day disorder; it was recognized by the Ancient Greeks. See *Anorexia nervosa*.

Bulla
A bubble or blister – from *bulla*, 'a bubble'. A bulla is the name given to any large blister, whether it be on the skin or possibly on the lungs, in the case of emphysema.

Bursa
A pouch or sac, usually pathological – from the Greek *bursa*, 'a wine skin'. Usually these are pouches forming near joints. They often become inflamed and produce symptoms, such as *prepatellar bursitis*, or housemaid's knee, or its counterpart at the elbow, *olecranon bursitis*.

C

Cacoethes loquendi

Compulsive talking – from the Greek *kakoethes*, meaning 'bad habit', and the Latin *loqui*, 'to speak'. This can occur to an almost pathological extent, thereby indicating the phenomenon of 'pressure of thought', characteristic of manic states. On the other hand some people are merely loquacious or natural chatterboxes.

Cacoethes scribendi

Compulsive writing – from the Greek *kakoethes*, meaning 'bad habit', and the Latin *scribere*, 'to write'. There are legions of scribblers around the world who burn to see their words in print. Compilers of trivia, crosswords and miscellanies such as this volume seem to be particularly badly affected.

Cadaver

A dead body – from *cadaver*, 'a corpse'. Cadaver is the scientific word for a dead human being, as opposed to the more lurid word of corpse. Medical students study anatomy by dissection of a cadaver. This is one of the ways that people generously help when they leave their body to science. Organs and other tissues (such as corneas) may be removed from a cadaver and used for transplantation into live patients, if the deceased has expressed a wish to leave body parts for organ donation. In the early nineteenth century the teaching of anatomy occupied a major part of medical education. The problem, however, was that there was an insufficient supply of cadavers to medical schools. As a result, the nefarious practice of body-snatching began. Unscrupulous people began digging up newly interred corpses and selling them illegally to medical schools. The perpetrators became known and feared as Resurrectionists. In the West Port of Edinburgh in 1827 William Burke and William Hare went a step further; they committed murder and then sold the cadaver to Dr Robert Knox at the Edinburgh Medical School. Dr Knox was a renowned anatomist and the Conservator of the Museum at the Royal College of Surgeons of Edinburgh. Reputedly, over the next year Burke and Hare murdered sixteen people and sold their bodies for dissection to the medical school, the main customer being Dr Knox. When the murderous pair were found out and brought to justice, Hare turned King's evidence and was spared, while Burke was sentenced to death by hanging followed by public dissection of his body by Professor Alexander Munro. The execution and public dissection took place in 1829, but apparently a disturbance occurred during the procedure and most of the skin that the professor had dissected away was stolen. Some weeks later wallets and pocket books of the tanned skin of William Burke were being sold on the black market. Dr Knox was never prosecuted, but his reputation was left in ruins. Ironically, it is recorded in the annals of Edinburgh University that Robert Knox failed his anatomy examination when he was a medical student. Following the Burke and Hare case the Anatomy Act of 1832 was passed by parliament. This allowed for the legal supply of cadavers for the purpose of research and education in order to stem the illegal trade in corpses.

Caduceus

The Latin word *caduceus* refers to the wand of the Greek god Hermes, known to the Romans as Mercury, the messenger of the gods. It was generally thought to be the symbol of the medical and related professions. There is confusion about this, however, since there are in fact two symbols used by different medical organizations, and other organizations have made adaptations of their own to indicate a particular feature of their calling. It is represented by a staff with two wings and two snakes coiled round it. In Roman days a white caduceus was used as a symbol of peace. From the sixteenth century it has been used as a symbol of the medical profession and it is now the adopted symbol of the US Army Medical Corps. The Faculty of Homeopathy in England also include it as part of its crest. The *Rod of Asclepius* is the other symbol and consists of a forked staff or rod with a single snake entwined about it. Asclepius was the Greek god of healing, whom the Romans adopted and called Aesculapius. The snake seems to have been a symbol of wisdom, fertility, regeneration and healing in Middle and Far Eastern countries, dating back to at least 2600 BCE. The snake associated with Asclepius is a species of rat-snake, *Elaphe longissima*, which is native to south-east Europe and Asia Minor. It is also found in areas of Germany and Switzerland, where it is thought the Romans introduced it at various health resorts. The Royal Society of Medicine, the British Medical Association and the American Medical Association use the Rod of Asclepius and a single snake as their logo, as does the World Health Organization. The Hungarian Pharmacy Association has modified this to have the Cup of Hygeia (the goddess of health, one of the two daughters of the god Asclepius) with the single snake curled about it. And the British Medical Acupuncture Society have adapted it by replacing the rod with an acupuncture needle on a background of the Yin and Yang symbol. Interestingly, *caduceus* was also an old name for epilepsy. See *Asclepius*.

Caecum
The first part of the large intestine, a blind cul-de-sac below the ileo-caecal valve, where the ileum, or the small intestine joins on to the large intestine. The appendix opens into the caecum. The Latin word *caecum* means 'a blind thing'.

Calcaneus
The heel bone – from *calcaneus*, 'about the heel'.

Calculus
Body stone – from *calculus*, 'limestone pebble'. Calculi can form in organs or ducts where body fluids pass through. You can develop them in salivary ducts, the gall bladder, the kidneys, bladder and ureters. They tend to cause pain because of blockage of flow of the fluids.

Calorie
A unit of heat and an indicator of the energy content of foods – from *calor*, 'heat'. Calor is also one of the four Roman signs of inflammation, first described by Celsus. See *Celsus*.

Calvaria
The skull cap, or the top of the skull, derived from *calvus* meaning 'bald'.

Cancer
The generic name given to malignant disease – from *cancer*, meaning 'crab'. The Ancient Greek physician

Galen described the crablike veins that spread out from a growth, and hence 'cancer' became associated with the disease. See *Galen*.

Candida albicans

A fungus that causes the common infection known as candidiasis or thrush – from *candidus*, meaning white and *albicans*, appertaining to white. The infection, whether in the vagina or the mouth, appears as areas of white on top of the normal mucus membranes. The name actually derives from the *toga candida*, or the white robe that was worn by members of the Roman senate.

Capiat

'Let the patient take.' In prescription-writing the abbreviation *cpt*.can be followed by some specific instruction which the doctor wants the pharmacist or chemist to write on the bottle of medicine or the pack of tablets. For example, 'cpt. after a loose bowel motion' when an anti-diarrhoeal preparation is prescribed.

Capsula

'A capsule.' In writing a prescription, the abbreviation *cap.* is used to indicate that a drug is to be given in capsule form.

Capsula amylacea

'A cachet, or a wafer capsule' to disguise unpleasant-tasting medication. These are not used much nowadays, because tablets are prepared so that their contents will be released in the stomach or further down the intestinal tract, and will not produce a taste. Modern coatings have taken away the need for this method of delivery.

Caput
Like the head – from *caput*, meaning 'head'. In anatomy this term is often used to describe part of a structure, as if it had a head. Hence, *caput coastae*, the head of a rib; *caput femoris*, the head of the thigh bone; *caput humerus*, the head of the upper arm bone.

Caput medusa
An interesting clinical sign in which obstruction of the inferior vena cava, a major blood vessel that returns blood to the heart, produces dilated blood vessels on the abdominal wall, like Medusa's head. The Medusa of Greek legend had once been a beautiful woman, but after offending the goddess Athena she was turned into a monster with hissing serpents replacing her once beautiful hair. Anyone who looked directly at her was turned into stone. Perseus slew her by making her see her own reflection.

Caput mortuum
'A death head, a skull.'

Cardiogenic syncope
A faint resulting from a problem with the heart – from the Greek *kardia*, heart and the Greek *gennan*, to produce, and syncope. See *syncope*.

Carmina
This word refers to odes, songs or poems. See *Horace*.

Carminative
A carminative is a medicine, such as peppermint oil, that eases flatulence or gas in the stomach and intestines. In very small children this gas may be the cause of colic.

Medical etymologists debate the origin of the word. It is thought to come from the Latin *carminare*, meaning 'to card wool', via the French *carminatif*. It has been suggested that the Latin *carminare* actually referred to 'cleansing' wool, and that a carminative would cleanse the bowel. The author of this work remains unconvinced by this and prefers the more poetic possibility, that it soothes the bowel, like a song or a good ode!

Carpus
The wrist – from *carpalis*, 'of the wrist'. There are eight small cubical bones in the wrist, called carpals, which are arranged in two rows. The proximal (nearest the centre of the body, therefore the ones at the forearm end) are: *scaphoid, lunate, triquetrum* and *pisiform*. The distal row (furthest from the centre of the body, at the hand end) are: *trapezium, trapezoid, capitate, hamate*. See individual bones, under *os – os scaphoideum*, etc.

Carotid artery
Main artery to the head and neck – from the Greek *karotides*, 'neck arteries'.

Cataplasma
'A poultice.' In prescription-writing the abbreviation *catplasm.* could indicate that a poultice was to be given, the particular ingredients of which would then follow on the prescription. For example, *cataplasma kaolini* – for a kaolin poultice.

Cataract
A clouding of the lens of the eye – from the Greek *kata*, 'down' and *rrhoia*, 'rushes'. A cataract develops as the lens of the eye becomes progressively opaque. It seems to

sufferers that a shutter or an obstruction is preventing them from seeing properly.

Catharsis

A clearing out – from the Greek *katharos*, 'clean' and *osis*, 'process of'. In psychiatry a catharsis is a flood of emotion, which seems then to be followed by a settling down.

Catullus

Gaius Valerius Catullus (circa 82 BCE–54 BCE) was born in Verona into an elite family. His father was a friend of Julius Caesar. However, Catullus more-or-less rebelled against his privileged position and devoted himself to poetry. In one poem *I, pete nobiles amicos* (So Much for Running after Powerful Friends!), he rants against nepotism and patronage. He belonged to the Neo-erotic poets who used colloquial language in their work. A large number of his poems analyse his feelings about the two great loves of his life, Clodia and Juventius.

Cauda equina

The horse's tail – from *cauda*, 'tail', and *equinus*, appertaining to a horse. The anatomical name given to the bundle of nerves that terminate the spinal cord. They do indeed resemble a horse's tail.

Cell

The smallest unit of body tissue – from *cella*, 'small room'. At conception a *spermatocyte* (the male reproductive cell) and an *oocyte* (the female reproductive cell, or egg) fuse together to form a *zygote*. This implants into the uterus and undergoes innumerable divisions and complex infoldings to produce a foetus. Continued development results in the birth of a baby or young human. Every cell of this young person will contain the same genetic information. It is estimated that the body of an adult human being is composed of between 75 to 100 trillion cells, of varying types and function. Similar cells make up tissues. It is also estimated that of this figure, about 40 trillion cells are not actually human, but consist of bacterial cells that live in the digestive system, and whose presence is necessary for our wellbeing. Of the human cells that make up the body, about a fifth make up the solid organs and tissues, the rest forming cells of the blood and lymph. There is a constant balance going on in the body between old cells dying off and new cells being produced to replace them. All of the red cells of the blood will have been replaced over a four-month period. It is also estimated that over a seven-year period all of the cells of the body will have been replaced. Each second, around one million cells die and are replaced. All in all you can see that there is plenty of scope for things to go wrong and for growth and repair to have difficulty keeping up with cell loss. And that, of course, is the process of ageing.

Celsus

Aulus Cornelius Celsus (25 BCE–AD 50) was a Roman encyclopedist and patrician, but is not thought to have been a doctor. Nonetheless, his only extant work, the *De Medicina*, is the only surviving section of a much larger encyclopedia. It is a primary source on diet, pharmacy and surgery and related fields. It was infuential for many centuries. Indeed, his description of the cardinal signs of inflammation: *calor* (warmth), *dolor* (pain), *tumor* (swelling) and *rubor* (redness) are still taught today. Celsus' work was rediscovered by Pope Nicholas V and in 1478 he became the first medical author to be printed in movable type after Gutenburg's invention.

Cerebellum
Literally, the small brain – from *cerebrum*, 'brain', and *ellum*, 'little'. The cerebellum is the lower part of the brain, which actually looks like a miniature version of the cerebrum. It coordinates movement and activity.

Cerebrum
The main part of the brain, consisting of the two cerebral hemispheres – from *cerebrum*, 'brain'. This is the part of the brain that coordinates the higher functions of the brain.

Cerumen
'Earwax.'

Cessante causa cessat et effectus
'When the cause is removed, the effect disappears.'
This would seem to be a good working principle in medicine. However, as any doctor of experience would tell you, removing the cause does not always remove the symptoms. It is a problem with many chronic illnesses.

Chlamydia
Chlamydia is the name of a genus of micro-organisms that are parasitic intra-cellular invaders. This means that they have to penetrate the cells of the organism they are infecting. The name comes from the Greek *chlamys*, which is the name that was given to an oblong cloak that was draped around the shoulders. This describes the sight that greets you on looking down the microscope at infected cells. The chlamydia can be seen draped around

the infected cell's nucleus, like a cloak. It is also appropriate in terms of the way it spreads, because it does so silently. Chlamydia is a sexually transmitted disease by the organism *Chlamydia trachomatis*. Respiratory infections can be caused by other members of the genus, *Chlamydia pneumoniae* or *Chlamydia psittacci*. The latter is contracted from inhaling the dried secretions from an infected bird, hence producing parrot fever. See *psittacosis*.

Cholecystectomy
Surgical operation to remove the gall bladder – from the Greek *chole*, 'bile', *kystis*, 'sac' or 'bladder', and *ectome*, 'removal of something'.

Cholesterol
A blood fat – from the Greek *chole*, 'bile', and *stereos*, 'solid'. It was originally thought that, because many gall stones were made out of cholesterol, it was simply solidified bile.

Chondromalacia patellae
Runner's knee – from the Greek *chondros*, 'cartilage', the Greek *malakia*, and the Latin *patellae*, 'of the kneecap'. This is a degenerative inflammation of the under-surface of the kneecap, common in runners and athletes.

Chronic
Long-lasting – from the Greek *chronikos*, 'taking time'. In medicine a chronic condition is one that has lasted a long time and might not be curable.

Cicatrix
'A scar.'

Cicero, Marcus Tullius

Marcus Tullius Cicero (*circa* 106 BCE–43 BCE) was an orator, lawyer, politician and statesman who lived in the tumultuous era that saw the decline and fall of the Roman republic. He himself played a significant part in that epoch and his writings are a valuable historical source for us. He placed politics above philosophical study. His works include: *Orationes (Orations), Rhetorica (Writings on Rhetoric), Philosophica (Political and Philosophical Writings)* and *Epistulae (Letters)*. At the end of his life he was declared an enemy of the state and forced to flee. He was caught and decapitated by his pursuers on 7 December 43 BCE. His head and hands were displayed on the Rostra in the Forum Romanum. According to Plutarch, the wife of one of his enemies pulled out his tongue, repeatedly stabbing it with a hatpin, taking a final revenge against Cicero's power of speech.

Cicero, Quintus

Quintus Tullius Cicero (*circa* 102 BCE–43 BCE) was a Roman general and the younger brother of Marcus Tullius Cicero, the orator. He accompanied Julius Caesar to Britain in 55 BCE. Together with his brother he was declared an enemy of the state and was killed with him.

Circumcision

Surgical removal of the foreskin – from the Latin *circum-cido*, 'I have cut around'.

Claustrophobia

Fear of enclosed spaces – from *claudere*, 'to shut', and the Greek *phobos*, 'fear'.

Clavicle
The collar-bone – from *clavicula*, 'little stick'. In anatomy, we also use the Greek *kleido* in composite words, which refer to the clavicle.

Clinic
Literally, 'a bed', from the Greek *kline*. Roman physicians used to teach at the bedside, such a lecture being called a *clinicus*.

Clitoris
An intensely sensitive bud of tissue just inside the vaginal entrance, at the apex of the Labii minora. From the Greek *kleitoris*, meaning 'key-user', or 'gatekeeper'. See *Labia*.

Coccyx
The tail bone – from the Greek *kokkygos*, 'the cuckoo'. This name comes from the appearance of the coccyx, which is not unlike the beak of a cuckoo.

Cochlea
The organ of hearing is situated in the internal ear. Its name comes from the Latin *cochlea* for 'snail's shell', which it resembles. It is supplied by the cochlear branch of the acoustic or vestibulocochlear nerve, and gives us the sense of hearing. Cochlear implants are sometimes used to give profoundly deaf people partial hearing.

Coeliac
Abdominal – from *coeliacus*, meaning 'abdominal'. Hence, the *coeliac trunk* is a major arterial branch from the abdominal aorta, which supplies part of the stomach and duodenum, liver, pancreas and spleen. The *coeliac plexus* (from plexus, meaning 'a braid') is a network of

nerves at the top of the abdomen. It is often referred to as the solar plexus, the target that boxers aim at to wind their opponent. *Coeliac disease* is a disorder of the intestines, as a result of an inability to handle gluten; the result being weight loss, abdominal pain, diarrhoea and failure to absorb nutrients. See *plexus* and *solar plexus*.

Cogito ergo sum
'I think, therefore I am.' The famous quotation of René Descartes. It sums up his attempt to prove the existence of one's self not through one's sense or experience but through reasoning alone. Some critics say that his logic is flawed, because he presupposes the 'I', in 'I think'. See *Descartes*.

Coitophobia
Male or female fear of heterosexual intercourse – from the Latin *coitus*, itself derived from *coire*, 'to come together', 'to copulate', and the Greek *phobos*, 'fear'.

Coitus
Sexual intercourse – from *coire*, 'to come together', 'to copulate'. This is the physical union of the male and female genitalia, which is accompanied by rhythmic movements of one or both partners, usually leading to the ejaculation of seminal fluid from the penis into the vagina. This is, of course, the bland biological description of coitus with a view to reproduction. Contraception involves the use of various agents or techniques to prevent conception taking place, thus freeing couples from the anxieties of unplanned pregnancy. The orgasm is the desirable end-point of love-making for most people. Writers in different cultures across the centuries have written extensively about the various ways in which couples can have intercourse and

foreplay in order to gain maximum mutual pleasure. The *Kama Sutra*, the famous Indian text, was written between the first and the sixth centuries, and is the book that people immediately think of when sex manuals are mentioned. In fact, the Roman poet Ovid wrote a three volume work, the *Ars Amatoria*, which is essentially a sex manual, between about 1 BCE and AD 1. See *Ovid*. Gender selection by employing various coital techniques has always been popular. In Roman days it was believed that the right testicle produced sperm which created male children, while the left produced females. Accordingly, bandaging one testicle was thought to allow the other a better chance of working to produce a child of the desired sex. It would of course have a 50 per cent chance of success.

Coitus interruptus
A form of family planning without the use of a contraceptive agent – literally, 'interrupted sex'. Commonly known as the withdrawal method.

Collunarium
'A nasal douche'. In prescription-writing the abbreviation *collun.* could be used to indicate that a nasal douche was to be dispensed.

Collutorium
'A mouthwash'. In prescription-writing the abbreviation *collut.* could be used to indicate that a mouthwash was to be dispensed.

Collyrium
'An eyewash'. In prescription-writing the abbreviation *coll.* could be used to indicate that an eyewash is to be dispensed.

Colon
The large intestine – from the Greek *kolon*. Aristotle coined this term for the large bowel, which starts at the right lower part of the abdomen and goes up to the base of the ribcage, travels across and then descends on the left side to the rectum.

Compos mentis
'Of sound mind.'

Confero
'I Compare.' This is often abbreviated to cf. in medical texts and papers.

Consilio manuque
'Scholarship and dexterity'. Motto of the Royal College of Surgeons of Ireland.

Contra malum mortis non est medicamen in hortis
'Against the evil of death there is no remedy in the garden (no herbal remedy).'

Contraria contrariis curantur
'Opposites are cured by their opposites.' This is said to be the basic philosophy of allopathic or orthodox medicine. It is the principle of fighting a disease with drugs that work against the symptoms of the illness. It is essentially the opposite of homoeopathic medicine. See *similia similibus curentur*.

Coprophilia
Sexual gratification involving faeces – from the Greek words *kopros*, 'dung', and *philia*, 'love'. This is one of the paraphilias. See *paraphilia*.

Coprophobia
Fear of faeces and bowel movements – from the Greek *kopros*, 'dung', and *phobos*, 'fear'. Sufferers from this phobia will go to great lengths to avoid seeing dung or faeces.

Cornea
The transparent outer shell of the eye that covers the iris and the pupil and is continuous with the sclera, the white of the eye. The name comes from the Latin *corneus*, meaning 'horny'.

Cornu
'Horn' – from the Latin *cornu*. The uterus is shaped like a pear. At the top of the uterus there are two hornlike protuberances where the fallopian tubes join the uterus. Each protuberance is called a *uterine cornu*. See also *stratum corneum*.

Corpori tantum indulgeas quantum bonae valetudini satis est
'Indulge the body so much as is enough for good health' – Seneca, (the younger) *Epistulae morales*, 8. See *Seneca*.

Corpse
A dead body – from *corpus*, 'body'. The word corpse entered the English language in the fourteenth century. It is the favoured word of sensationalist literature and crime fiction, rather than cadaver. Sometimes the word carcass is used to refer to the dead body of an animal or bird.

Corpus callosum
A part of the brain – from *corpus*, 'body', and *callosum*, meaning 'hard parts'. This is the largest white-matter

part of the mammalian brain. It mostly consists of nerve fibres crossing from the opposite side of the brain. It is extremely important because it connects the left and right cerebral hemispheres.

Corpus cavernosum
An important part of the penis (and the clitoris), especially for the purposes of having an erection – from *corpus*, 'body', and *cavernosum*, meaning 'full of cavities'. This is essentially the bulk of the shaft of the penis, which is full of cavities that fill with blood during an erection. You cannot actually consider an erection fully – or full – until you also consider what happens in the other parts of the penis, the *corpus spongiosum* and *glans penis*. See *corpus spongiosum* straight away.

Corpus curare spiritumque
'To care for the body and its breath of life.' Motto of the Australian and New Zealand College of Anaesthetists.

Corpus delicti
'The evidence of a crime.' A legal term, also of relevance in medical jurisprudence.

Corpus Hippocraticum
The Hippocratic corpus is a library, or rather the remains of a library, attributed to Hippocrates. It consists of thirty-four books, which scholars now believe to have been written by several authors between the sixth and fourth centuries BCE. Hippocrates probably did write about eight of the books, which make remarkable reading even today.

Corpus onustum hesternis vitiis animum quoque praegravat una

'The body, weighed by the excesses of yesterday, depresses the intellect at the same time' – Horace, *Satires* book 2, 2, 77. See *Horace*.

Corpus spongiosum

The spongy part of the penis – from *corpus*, 'body', and *spongiosum*, 'spongelike'. The *corpus spongiosum* runs the length of the penis and merges with the mushroomlike glans penis. The urethra, the tube from the bladder, runs through it. During an erection this spongelike tissue fills with blood and elongates the penis and fills up the *glans penis* like a little balloon.

Craniosacral osteopathy

A complementary therapy and a discipline of the manipulative therapy of osteopathy. It involves very subtle manipulation of the cranial skull bones and the bones of the sacrum. Quite remarkable results seem to have been obtained across a range of conditions.

Cras mane

'Tomorrow morning'. In prescription-writing the abbreviation *c.m.* could be used to indicate that a particular remedy is to be taken on the following morning. It is likely that it would be a one-off remedy.

Cras vespere

'Tomorrow evening'. In prescription-writing the abbreviation *c.v.* could be used to indicate that a particular remedy is to be taken on the following evening. It is likely that it would be a one-off remedy.

Cum corpore et una crescere sentimus; pariterque senescere mentem

'We feel the mind growing with the body, and equally ageing with it' – Lucretius, *De Rerum Natura*, 3, 446. See *Lucretius*.

Cum scientia caritas

'Scientific knowledge applied with compassion.' Motto of the Royal College of General Practitioners.

Cunnilingus

Oral sex performed on a female. Literally 'he who licks the vulva', from New Latin *cunnus*, 'vulva', and *lingere*, 'to lick'. See *Vulva*.

Cura te ipsum

'Cure thyself.' See *medice, cura te ipsum*.

Cura ut valeas

'Be careful of your health' – Cicero, *Epistulae*, 7, 5. See *Cicero*.

Curriculum vitae

'Course of life.' A curriculum vitae is a resumé of one's educational attainments, work record and interests, generally required when applying for posts.

D

Dacryocystitis
Inflammation and blockage of the tear duct – from the Greek *dakryon*, 'tear', and the Greek *kystis*, 'sac'. This condition will usually settle with special drops, but may require more active intervention to unblock the ducts.

Dactylomegaly
Excessively large fingers and toes – from the Greek words *daktylos*, 'finger', and *megale*, 'enlargement'. This is often a sign of the condition acromegaly, due to excess growth hormone.

Decubitus hora
At bedtime – from *de*, 'from', *cubitus*, 'lying in bed', and *hour of*. In prescription-writing the abbreviation *decub.hora.* could be used when some medication has to be used at bedtime.

Decubitus ulcer
A bedsore – from the Latin *de*, 'from', *cubitus*, 'lying in bed', and *ulcus*, 'sore'.

De Humani Corporis Fabrica
On the Fabric of the Human Body – a revolutionary textbook of anatomy by Andreas Vesalius (1543). See *Vesalius*.

Delirium
To go off the track, to lose the logical path, to be slightly

mad – from *de*, 'away', and *lira*, 'ploughed furrow' – hence it meant to lose the plot, to be mad. Delirium is to lose touch with reality and become confused, to be not really conscious. It is an acute confusional state that can come about through injury, severe infection or intoxication.

Delirium tremens
Trembling madness – from *delirium* and *tremens*, 'trembling'. This is a severe withdrawal effect in alcoholics. They get the 'DTs', shake, and become agitated and confused.

Dementia
This is a deterioration of intellectual faculties, such as memory, concentration, and judgement, as a result of an organic disease or a disorder of the brain. It is sometimes accompanied by emotional disturbance and personality changes. It comes from the Latin *demens*, senseless, or madness. Several types of dementia are recognized these days, of which Alzheimer's disease is the commonest.

Dementia praecox
This is the old name for the mental condition of schizophrenia. It comes from *dementia* and *praecox*, 'premature'. The term is no longer used but is of historical interest.

Dementia senilis
This is the old name for dementia occurring in older ages. Several types are recognized, of which Alzheimer's disease is the commonest these days. The term is no longer used, but comes from *dementia* and *senilis*, 'of old age'.

De novo
'Anew, a fresh start.' In medicine it means newly synthesized, hence a newly synthesized molecule or protein.

Depressor anguli oris
The sulking muscle – literally, the muscle that presses down the angle of the mouth.

Depressor muscles
Muscles which press down – from *de*, 'away', and *premere*, 'to press'.

Descartes
The French philosopher René Descartes (1596–1650) is considered by many to be the father of modern philosophy. He was the first scientist-philosopher to organize the process of thought and link it to the meaning of one's very existence. This is embodied in his famous argument, *cogito ergo sum* – 'I think, therefore I am'. He is famous for developing the concept of Cartesian dualism: the view that mind and body are separate, distinct substances. He believed that the tools of science and mathematics could be used to explain and predict events in the physical world. Reductionism, the belief that complex things or systems can be understood by being reduced to simple things or simple component systems, was a natural result. In many ways, modern medicine is reductionist in its philosophy. An alternative movement is embodied in the concept of holism, the belief that things as a whole can have properties that are not explainable from the properties of their parts. The behaviour of bees and wasps in showing 'swarm intelligence' is a good example of holism in a biological system. See *cogito ergo sum*.

Desquamation
Scaling – from *de*, 'away', and *squama*, 'fish or snake scale'. Desquamation or scaling of the skin is normal.

The squamous cells of the skin are flat, scale-like cells and they do slide off, when they die. Excessive scaling occurs after sunburn and in various skin ailments.

Dextra manu
'With the right hand.'

Diabetes mellitus
'The honey-sweet siphon.' A disorder of carbohydrate metabolism from too little insulin or from a lack of response to the body's own insulin. The characteristic feature of it in an undiagnosed or untreated form is excess thirst and increased tendency to pass urine. Medical writers have been aware of the condition for at least 4,000 years. It is mentioned in the Ebers Papyrus, an Egyptian text from 1550 BCE. Aretaeus first used the word diabetes in AD 100 to indicate this condition (*dia*, meaning 'through', and *betes* meaning 'passing'), likening the passing through of urine to a siphon action. Thomas Willis, personal physician to King Charles II, stated that diabetic urine was 'wonderfully sweet as if it were imbued with Honey or Sugar', because tasting patients' urine was an art that most physicians practised. (I am so glad that they have invented test-strips these days, so I don't have to 'take the piss'!) He added the Latin word *mellitus*, meaning 'honey sweet'.

Diagnosis
Find the answer, find the cause – from the Greek *dia*, 'through' and the Greek *gnosis*, 'knowledge'. Diagnosis is the name given to the process of identifying the disease or illness from which a patient is suffering, in order to understand how it is likely to progress, and in order to discover its cause. This process takes into

account the symptoms that the patient is experiencing by taking a case history, and by eliciting signs from a physical examination, and by performing various tests. These may range from blood tests, to microbiological examination of body fluids, X-rays and other more sophisticated types of imaging. Once the information has been gathered, a differential diagnosis is constructed, which is essentially a league table of the main diagnostic possibilities. The main diagnosis is reached after the others have been excluded and the body of evidence considered sufficient to justify the main diagnosis. Then a treatment regime and management plan can be worked out. Cf. *prognosis*.

Diarrhoea

Loose bowel motions – from the Greek words *dia*, 'through' and *rrhoia*, 'a flowing'. Diarrhoea is the passage of excessive, loose, almost fluid, bowel motions. It is very common and most people will suffer from it at some time in their life. Usually, it is caused by a virus or bacteria, and normally it is a self-limiting ailment. If it is so severe that it causes dehydration, however, then it can be extremely dangerous, necessitating hospitalization and the administration of intravenous fluids. It is often caused by an infection transmitted by drinking contaminated water or fluid, undercooked meat or eggs, or as the result of inadequate kitchen hygiene. If it persists for more than a few days, if the individual feels ill or if there is blood present in the diarrhoeal fluid, then medical assistance should be sought. Globally, seven children die every minute as the result of diarrhoeal illnesses. The majority of these cases occur in the underdeveloped countries where contaminated water and malnutrition are still major problems.

Diebus alternis
'Every other day.' In prescription-writing the abbreviation *dieb. alt.* could be used when something is to be taken or done on alternate days.

Digastric muscle
The two-bellied muscle – from the Greek *di*, 'two', and *gaster*, 'belly'. This small muscle under the jaw has two different bellies. One of its main functions is to open the jaw.

Digitalis purpurea
'Foxglove.' See *hydrops*.

Dilator naris
Small muscles that help widen the nostrils. Some people can really flare their nostrils when angered or when something 'gets up their nose'.

Dilator pupillae
The radially arranged muscle fibres in the iris of the eye which open the pupil when light is failing or when an 'object of desire' (or 'person of desire') is in the vicinity!

Dioscorides
Pedanius Dioskorides, known to history simply as Dioscorides (AD 40–90) was an ancient Greek physician, surgeon and botanist who practised in Rome at the times of the emperors Nero and Trajan. Because he was an army surgeon he travelled extensively and was able to gain experience of many medicinal substances from all over the Roman and Greek world. He wrote a five-volume book *De Materia Medica*, which is a precursor to all modern pharmacopeias and is one of the most influ-

ential herbal books in history. It remained in use until about 1600.

Dividatur in partes aequales

'Divide into equal parts.' In prescription-writing the abbreviation *div. in part aequ.* could be used when an instruction is being given to divide something, be it a tablet or powder, into equal parts.

Divinum sedare dolorem

'It is divine (or praiseworthy) to relieve pain.' Motto of the Royal College of Anaesthetists.

Doctor

A teacher – from *docere*, 'to teach'. The title of doctor has been used throughout Europe for about a millennium, as an academic title, for anyone who holds a higher degree or doctorate, e.g. Doctor of Philosophy, PhD; Doctor of Science, DSc; Doctor of Medicine, MD; doctor of Law, LLD, etc. Over the last two centuries the honorary title of doctor has come to be associated with the profession of medicine, even though the qualifying degrees in the UK are not doctorates, but conjoint Bachelor degrees, such as MB ChB. Most medical practitioners are conscious of the meaning of the word doctor, and accept that a doctor essentially has to teach his patients how to keep healthy and how to deal with their illness. See *Medicinae Baccalaureus – Baccalaureus Chirurgia* and *Medicinae Doctoris*.

Doctrine of Humors

The Ancient Greeks developed the Doctrine of Humors as an explanation of health and disease. It was a theory that dominated medical thinking until the Renaissance. Essentially, it was believed that there were four fundamental humors or body fluids (from the Latin *umor* or *humor*, meaning 'moisture' or 'fluid') which determined the state of health of the individual. These humors were blood, yellow and black bile and phlegm. Aristotle had taught that the humors were associated with the four elements of air, fire, earth and water, which in turn were associated with the paired qualities of hot, cold, dry and moist. Thus, earth would be dry and cold, water would be wet and cold, fire would be hot and dry, and air would be wet and hot. He postulated that this association allowed for the transformation of one element into another, if the predominance of one quality was altered. For example, fire, which is dry and hot, plus water, which is wet and cold, could respectively lose dryness and coldness to form earth, which is cold and dry, and air, which is wet and hot. A proper balance of the humors was considered characteristic of a healthy body and mind. An excess of any humor could be treated by reducing a quality, or by reducing a humor, for instance by bleeding the patient or giving enemas, or treating with various Gallenical drugs. The individual's temperament could also be discerned according to his or her balance of humors. Thus, sanguine individuals were perceived to have excess blood, choleric individuals had excess yellow bile, melancholics had too much black bile and phlegmatics had excess phlegm. As a philosophical system it has much to commend it, and it is in fact often still used in the system of medicine called Unani in India, and in various complementary systems of medicine. See *Galenical*.

Doctrine of signatures

Since the beginnings of time man has believed that plants are marked with a divine sign indicating their medicinal purpose. For example, the white-spotted leaves of the lungwort (*Pulmonaria officinalis*) resemble a diseased lung and this was thought to indicate the plant's ability to deal with lung problems. The Ancient Egyptian Ebers papyrus (*circa* 1550 BCE) gives examples of the doctrine of signatures, as do the writings of Galen. The first use of the term the doctrine of signatures is found in the book *Signatura Rerum* (*Signature of All Things*) by Jakob Boehme (1575–1624), a master shoemaker of Goerlitz, Germany.

Dolor
'Pain.'

Dolor animi gravior est quam corporis
'Pain of the mind is worse than pain of the body' – Pubilius Syrus. See *Syrus, Pubilius*.

Dolor urgente
'While the pain is severe.' In prescription-writing the abbreviation *dol. urg.* could be used when a remedy or application is to be used until a painful condition begins to settle down.

Dorsum
'The back.' In anatomy the dorsum is the back side of the body, as opposed to the ventral side, the front.

Duct
'A canal' – from the Latin *ductus*. In anatomy this refers to any tubular structure that carries a body fluid. For example, tear ducts, bile and pancreatic ducts.

Duodenum
The twelve fingerbreadths long intestine – from *duodenum digitorum*, meaning 'twelve fingers breadth'.

The duodenum is a loop that joins the stomach to the jejunum. Inside the loop is the pancreas. It was named thus because it is on average twelve fingerbreadths long.

Durante dolore
'While the pain lasts.' In prescription-writing the abbreviation *dur.dol.* could be used when a remedy has to be taken until a pain goes.

E

Edere oportet ut vivas, non vivere ut edas
'You ought to eat to live, not live to eat' – Cicero. See *Cicero*.

Edo, ergo sum
'I eat, therefore I exist.' An old Roman proverb, at variance with the later famous philosophical expostulation of René Descartes. See *cogito ergo sum* and *Descartes* .

Ego and Superego
Ego – 'I, me'. In Freud's view the Ego stands in between the Id and the Superego to balance our primitive needs and our moral beliefs and taboos. He taught that the Superego represented our conscience and counteracted the Id with a primitive and unconscious sense of morality. See *Freud, Id*.

Embolus
A plug of fat or blood clot lodging in a blood vessel – from the Greek *embolos*, 'a plug'.

Embryo
The developing product of conception – from the Greek *em*, 'in', and *bryon*, 'growing thing'.

Emeritus
'Honorary; by merit.' A consultancy or an academic post is often given or held on an honorary basis.

Emetic

A drug or agent that induced vomiting – from Greek *emetikos*, 'regarding vomiting'. If someone has inadvertently, or deliberately taken a poisonous substance, or too much of a prescription drug, then emesis, the inducement of vomiting may be needed on therapeutic grounds.

Emmenagogue

A drug or agent that induces or hastens menstrual flow – from Greek *emmena*, 'the monthly flow', and *agogos*, 'leading to something'.

Emollient

A substance used externally to soften and relax tissues and to soothe the part it is applied to – from *emollire*, 'to soften'.

Emotion

'Feelings' – from *'emovere*, 'to excite'. An emotion is a mental state that arises unconsciously rather than through conscious effort, and which is often accompanied by physiological or bodily sensations. It is sometimes regarded as the opposite of reason, for there is sometimes no logic in the emotions we experience or feel. There are the positive emotions of love, joy, pleasure, happiness, and less positive emotions such as sadness, fear, anger, hate, guilt and jealousy. Sometimes emotions seem interrelated. It is said that love makes the world go round, but hate makes it spin. And jealousy, as defined by Spinoza is a '... mixture of hate and love.'

Endocardium

Inside lining tissue of the heart – from the Greek *endon*, 'within', and *kardia*, 'heart'.

Endolymphatic hydrops

Endolymphatic hydrops is a disorder of the vestibular system of the inner ear. It stems from abnormal fluctuations in the fluid called endolymph, which fills the hearing and balance structures of the inner ear. It is commonly known as Ménière's disease and is associated with the triad of symptoms: deafness, tinnitus and dizziness.

Endometrium

Inside lining of the womb – from the Greek *endon*, 'within', and *metra*, 'mother' (organ).

Enterobius vermicularis

Threadworms or pinworms – from the Greek *enteron*, 'gut', *bios*, 'living', and the Scientific Latin *vermicularis*, derived from *vermiculus* 'small worm' – literally 'the small worms that live in the gut'. Threadworms are common in up to forty per cent of the under tens at any one time. The worms live in the intestine and come out to lay eggs on the bottom at night.

Epilepsy

A seizure – from *epilesis*, 'a seizure'. Epilepsy has been recognized for several millennia. The ancients believed it to be an affliction sent by the gods and called it the 'sacred disease'. The Greek physician Hippocrates, however, made a study of the condition and wrote a book about it in about 400 BCE, entitled *On the Sacred Disease*. In it he refuted the idea that it had a divine origin, but felt that it was a disorder of the brain. Nowadays epilepsy is accepted as a general term for a group of disorders that cause disturbance in the electrical activity of the brain. Ordinarily, the brain's electrical system is powered by pulses of energy taking place at about eighty pulses a second. An epileptic seizure occurs when the pulses fire off at a rate up to 500 per second, in some electrically abnormal part of the brain. As a result, this surge of electrical activity, dependent upon which part or parts of the brain are being affected, can cause alterations in the individual's awareness of their body, or their state of consciousness, and it may cause uncontrolled movements of part or the whole of the body. Modern medicine has much to offer the individual with this condition.

Eripit interdum, modo dat medicina salutem
Medicine sometimes snatches away health, sometimes gives it – Ovid, *Tristia*, 2, 269. See *Ovid*.

Errare humanum est
'It is human to err' – and it is recognized that doctors are only too human. However, the Hippocratic code quite correctly insists that all doctors must at all time behave ethically in their dealings with their patients.

Erythrism
This is the trait of red hair – from the Greek *erythrismos*, 'redness'.

Erythrocyte
A red blood cell – from the Greek *erythros*, 'red', and *kytos*, meaning 'hollow', nowadays translated as cell.

Erythromycin
A group of broad-spectrum antibiotics, named from the Greek *erythros*, 'red' and the Greek *mykes*, meaning 'fungus' or 'mushroom'. Essentially, erythromycin is

produced by the bacterium *Streptomyces erythreus*, which was originally extracted from a red mushroom.

Erythropoiesis
The process whereby red blood cells are produced in the bone marrow – from the Greek *erythros*, 'red', and the Greek *poiesis*, meaning 'creation'.

Essential
In a medical context this means occurring *idiopathically*, without a known cause – from *essentia*, 'the essence of'. It has a quite different meaning compared to the 'essential' of common parlance, which means that something is indispensable. For example, *essential hypertension* is the name given to the common type of hypertension, or raised blood pressure. It seems to arise without any obvious cause.

Et al.
And others – from *et alii* (masculine form: 'other men'), *et aliae* (feminine form: 'other women') and *et alia* (neutral form: 'other things'). This is commonly used in scientific papers, when referring to a list of authors of a paper. After the principal author's name the abbreviation et al. may be added to indicate 'and other authors'. Their names would be cited in full in the referenced work.

Etiam sanato vulnere cicatrix manet
'Even when the wound is healed the scar remains.'

Eugenics
Literally, 'good-breeding'. This philosophy has been controversial since it was first postulated by Sir Francis Galton in 1865. It became associated with various social policies that fell into the two categories of positive

eugenics – the encouragement of the 'fittest' to repro-
duce, and negative eugenics – the discouragement of
reproduction by the 'less fit'. In the twentieth century the
concept became associated with the disgusting policies
of the Nazis and their belief in a master race.

Euphoria
Good spirits, well-being – from *eu*, 'well' and the Greek
phoros, 'carriage', means literally 'well carriage', and that
one feels well. To have good spirits and a sense of well-
being is desirable for everyone. In medicine, however,
the presence of excessive euphoria always has to be
taken seriously, since it can be indicative of bipolar
disorder, or of the condition formerly known as manic-
depression.

Eustachian tube
See *pharyngotympanic tube*.

Eustachi, Bartolomeo
The Italian anatomist and physician Bartolomeo Eustachi
(1513–74) is considered by many to be the premier
comparative anatomist of the Renaissance. He was the
first to describe the teeth in detail, including their basic
composition of enamel and dentin. He published the first
accounts of the adrenal gland and thoracic duct as well as
the first accurate description of the auditory tube, or
pharyngotympanic tube, that was dubbed the 'Eustachian
tube' in his honour. This tube links the middle ear to the
throat. See *anatomy* and *pharyngotympanic tube*.

Euthanasia
Literally 'good death' – from *eu*, 'well', 'good', and the
Greek *thanatos*, 'death'. Everyone would surely wish to

have a good, painless death when their time comes. However, we cannot choose how our end will come, which is why campaigners in different countries are trying to persuade governments and legal systems to permit active measures to terminate life as someone approaches death. The ethical issues involved are collossal.

Ex aqua
'With water.' In prescription-writing the abbreviation *ex.aq.* could be used when a drug has to be taken with water.

Ex aquae cyatho vinario
'In a wineglass of water.' In prescription-writing the abbreviation *ex. aq. cyath. vin.* could be used when something, usually a powder or drops is to be added to a larger amount of water, classically a wineglass measure. People were more sophisticated in days gone by.

Excessit medicina malum
'The remedy has exceeded the disease.' It is a basic principle in therapy that one should not overtreat. Sometimes a treatment can be given or taken for too long, with the result that another condition develops. For example, *rhinitis medicamentosa* is a congestive condition of the nose that can come about from overlong use of nasal medications and sprays.

Excision
Cut out surgically – from *excidere*, 'to cut away'. Many lesions are surgically excised if it is felt that their continued presence in the body could do harm. Malignant tumours or growths are often excised together with surrounding tissue and draining lymph nodes.

Similarly, damaged tissue that may become infected and turn gangrenous after injuries is excised.

Exercitato anatomica de motu cordis et sanguinis in animalibus

'An anatomical disquisition on the movements of the heart and blood in animals' – the title of the ground-breaking book by William Harvey about the circulation of the blood. See *Harvey, William*.

Ex modo prescripto

'Give as directed, or as prescribed.' In prescription-writing the abbreviation *e.m.p.* could be used to indicate that the medicine is to be given as directed by the doctor.

Exophthalmos

Protuberance of the eyes, usually a sign of the condition hyperthyroidism – from the Latin *ex*, 'out', and the Greek *ophthalmos*, 'eye'.

Extensor muscles

Muscles that extend or stretch – from *extendere*, 'to stretch'. There are five extensor muscles that open the hand and which pull back the toes. In the arm they extend from the outer side of the elbow and are inserted into each of the digits (from thumb to little finger): *extensor pollicis longus*, *extensor carpi radialis*, *extensor pollicis brevis*, *extensor digitorum*, and *extensor digiti minimi*. When these muscles are overworked by repetitive strain, then the outer point of the elbow becomes painful and inflamed, as the condition tennis elbow.

F

Facies
The face. This is the general anatomical term for the face, but different facial presentations can indicate different states, or clinical conditions:

Facies abdominalis – an anxious, pinched face with furrowed brow in someone experiencing severe abdominal pain.

Facies Hippocratica – someone with a pinched expression, with sunken eyes, hollow cheeks and temples, and relaxed lips. Hippocrates himself described this, saying that it was characteristic of one dying after an exhausting illness. See *Hippocrates*.

Facile omnes, cum valemus, recta concilia aegrotis damus
'When we are well we all easily give good advice to the sick' – Terence, *Andria*, 2, 1, 11. See *Terence*.

Faeces
Stools, or bowel motions – from *faecis*, meaning 'dung'. Faeces is the name used in medicine for the excreta from the digestive tract. The colour, texture, form and bulk may all have significance in various conditions. Doctors test for occult (hidden or digested) blood, fat content, presence of various parasites and their eggs, bacteria and viruses.

Fascia
Connective tissue under the skin that protects the underlying tissues. From *fascia*, meaning 'band' or 'bandage'.

Fasciitis
The condition when fascia becomes inflamed. For example, the fascia padding of the heel becomes inflamed and acutely painful in plantar fasciitis, commonly known as policeman's heel.

Fasciola hepatica
'Liver fluke'.

Fax mentis incendium gloriae
'The torch that illuminates the mind is the fire that consumes vainglory.' Motto of the Royal Australian College of Surgeons.

Febrifuge
Old name for a medicine that lowers a fever – from *febris*, 'burning', and *fugere*, 'to flee', 'to drive away'. Nowadays the word 'pyrexia' is used instead of 'fever' and 'anti-pyretic' is used instead of 'febrifuge'. See *fever, pyrexia* and *anti-pyretic*.

Fellatio
Oral stimulation of the penis – from New Latin *fellatus*, from fellare, 'to suck'.

Femur
The thigh bone – from *femur*, 'the thigh'. The largest bone in the body, and the strongest. Its rounded head fits into the socket of the pelvis, the acetabulum, to form a ball and socket joint. See *acetabulum*.

Fever

A high temperature – from *fervere*, 'to be hot', 'to boil'. Feverish illnesses are common and there are many causes. In the past the main causes were infectious. In the fifth century BCE, Hippocrates classified the fever types as *quotidian* (daily), *tertian* (alternate days) and *quartan* (fever three days apart). He also noticed that those who lived near swamps or marshes and who drank stagnant water had large stiff spleens, a characteristic of the disease that they called swamp fever. Nowadays we call it malaria. Generally, we tend to use the word pyrexia instead of fever nowadays. See *pyrexia*, *anti-pyretic* and *febrifuge*.

Fiat

'Let it be made.' In prescription-writing the abbreviation *ft*. might be used as an indication to the pharmacist that a remedy is to be made up with certain ingredients.

Fibula

The smaller of the two bones of the lower leg – from *fibula*, 'brooch-pin'. Fibula itself is derived from *figere*, 'to fasten'. The fibula rests beside the larger tibia, and resembles a brooch fastener or pin.

Flatus

Bowel wind – from the Latin word *flatus*, 'wind'. This is the presence of air or gas in the lower bowel, and its passage. In common parlance, to pass flatus is 'to fart'.

Flexor muscles

Bending muscles – from *flectere*, 'to bend'. The flexor muscles bend joints. There are several fine muscles that flex or bend the wrist and hand to make a fist, including:

flexor carpi radialis, flexor digitorum superficialis, flexor carpi ulnaris and *palmaris longus*.

Foetus
The developing baby inside the womb – from *fetus*, 'spawn'.

Foramen
A hole, or aperture – from the word *foramen*, meaning 'hole'. In anatomy a foramen represents a hole in a bone through which vital structures pass.

Foramen magnum
The big hole – from *foramen*, 'hole' and *magnum*, 'big'. The large hole at the back of the skull, through which the spinal cord passes.

Foramen ovale
The oval hole. Before birth a connection called the *foramen ovale* exists between the right and the left sides of the heart and allows blood to bypass the lungs. Usually this connection closes after birth, but in some people it fails to close, resulting in a patent foramen ovale, or a hole in the heart.

Forceps
Surgical instrument – from the Latin word *forceps*, meaning 'tongs'. The first forceps were actually rather heavy tools used by blacksmiths. Later, smaller variants were used to pull teeth. As time passed and they became adapted for surgical purposes a whole variety of different forceps were developed. Nowadays we use very fine and coarse 'toothed' forceps which allow the operator to 'bite' into tissue with the instrument to hold it steady during an

operation. Also, we use mosquito forceps to nip off bleeding blood vessels at an operation. In obstretrics much larger forceps are used to deliver babies. Although various types of forceps were used in medieval times the forerunner of the modern obstretrical instruments was developed by the Chamberlain family in the early seventeenth century. They were famed accoucheurs who kept their forceps a secret for many years. Doctors often refer to their obstretic forceps as 'forks!'

Forensic anthropology
The identification of human remains in medico-legal cases – from forensic and the Greek words *anthropos*, 'man', and *logos*, 'the study of something'.

Forensic archaeology
The excavation of medical remains in medico-legal cases – from forensic and the Greek words *archaios*, 'ancient' and *logos*, 'the study of something'.

Forensic entomology
The study of insects found around or on dead bodies from forensic and the Greek words *entomon*, 'insect', and *logos*, 'the study of something'. The type of insects and their state of development, in combination with weather data and the condition of a decomposing body, can provide forensic investigators with accurate indicators of time of death.

Forensic medicine
The branch of medicine dealing with the law – *forensis*, 'a court or forum'. In ancient Rome the forum was a market place where people gathered, not just to buy things, but also to conduct all kinds of business, including that of

public affairs. The meaning of *forensic* later came to be restricted to refer to the courts of law. The word entered English usage in 1659.

Forensic odontology

The identification of a dead person through a dental examination and the examination of teeth from forensic and the Greek words *odontos*, 'tooth', and *logos*, 'the study of something'.

Fossa

In anatomy a *fossa*, from the Latin for 'trench or ditch', refers to a depression in an organ, tissue or bone, into which another part fits. For example, the olecranon fossa at the back of the base of the humerus (the upper arm bone) receives the olecranon (the point of the elbow) of the ulna. See *olecranon*.

Fracture

A break – from the Latin word, *fractura*, 'a breaking'. Trauma and injury has always been a problem for mankind and is still one of the largest causes of mortality and morbidity in the world today. The management of fractures or broken bones was studied and written about by the Indian surgeon Sushrutha in about 400 BCE, at the same time that the Greek physician Hippocrates also wrote a work on the subject. The discipline of orthopaedics combines carpentry techniques with the highest technology to fix the most complicated of fractures, and to replace most of the joints of the body.

Frenulum

'A fold or small ligament' that tethers a body part to deeper tissue. For example, there is the *lingual frenulum* that tethers the lip to the gums, and there is the *penile frenulum*, which tethers the foreskin to the penis.

Freud

Sigmund Freud (1856–1939) was an Austrian neurologist and the founder of the psychoanalytic school of psychology. At first he used hypnosis in his work with patients, but later developed his method of analysis by free association. He started a movement that popularized the theory that unconscious motives control much behaviour. Much of our unconscious motivation, he believed, is to do with sexual needs, desires and repressed thoughts. His theories of the interaction of Id, Ego and Superego had a profound effect on Western thought for many decades. He escaped Nazi Germany in 1937. See *Ego and Superego*, *Id* and *Lapsus linguae*.

G

Galen

Claudius Galenus of Pergamum (AD 131–201), better known as Galen, was an Ancient Greek physician whose views and teachings dominated European medicine for over a thousand years. At the age of twenty he became an apprentice Asclepiad, a doctor. He studied in Smyrna and Corinth and at Alexandria, returning to Pergamum (in modern day Turkey) in AD157, where he worked as a physician in a gladiator school. During this time he gained valuable experience in trauma work. Indeed, he was to write that wounds were 'windows into the body'. He eventually became physician to Emperor Marcus Aurelius, and later to Lucius Verus, Commodus and Septimius Severus. Galen was the first real anatomist, who performed numerous dissections on different species of animals. He also wrote extensively on the Doctrine of Humors, which was to be the dominant philosophy of medicine for centuries. See *anatomy* and *Doctrine of Humors*.

Galenical

A drug used after the fashion of Galen. Essentially, Galenicals were drugs designed to correct imbalance in the body humours. Excess heat, for example, would require a cooling Galenical. The common vegetable cucumber was such a cooling Galenical. A hint of this is contained in the common phrase 'as cool as a cucumber'.

Indeed, analysis of cucumber reveals that it has salicylate-like qualities, which are indeed cooling. See *Doctrine of Humors*.

Gangrene
Tissue death – from the Greek *gangraina*, meaning 'ulcer that kills tissue'. Gangrene is the name for death of tissue, when the blood supply is impaired.

Gargarisma
A gargle. In prescription-writing the abbreviation *garg.* may be used when a gargle is to be dispensed for a painful condition of the throat.

Gastric
To do with the stomach – from the Greek *gaster*, meaning 'belly' or 'stomach'.

Gastrocnemius
The calf muscle – from the Greek *gaster*, 'belly' and *kneme*, 'leg', literally, the 'belly of the leg'. The large muscle that becomes the Achilles tendon.

Genioglossus
One of the deep muscles of the tongue – from the Greek words, *geneion*, 'chin', and *glossa*, 'tongue'. There is a genioglossus muscle at each side of the tongue. To see its profound effect, stick your tongue out at somebody. That's just one of the things it can do.

Genu
The knee – from the Latin *genu* for 'knee'. *Genu valgum* – 'knock-knees' and *genu varum* – 'bow legs'.

Geriatrics

The medical specialty dealing with the elderly – from the Greek *geron*, 'old person', and *iatros*, 'doctor'.

Glossal

To do with the tongue – from the Greek *glossa*, 'the tongue'.

Gluteus maximus

The large buttock muscle – from the Greek *gloutos*, 'buttock', and the Latin *maximus*, 'largest'. The large muscle that gives shape to the bottom. It is one of three gluteal muscles, the others being *gluteus medius* and *gluteus minimus*.

Gonad

Sex organ – either the male testis or the female ovary – from New Latin *gonas*, 'seed store'.

Gonococcus and Gonorrhoea

The bacterium, *Neisseria gonorrhoeae*, which causes the sexually transmitted disease, gonorrhoea: the gonococcus is a diplococcus, meaning that it is a paired coccus. See *bacteria*.

Graviora quaedam sunt remedia periculis

'Some remedies are worse than the dangers.'

Gutta, guttae

'A drop, drops.' In prescription-writing the abbreviation *gtt.* or *gutt.* is used when eyedrops are prescribed.

Gynaecology

The study of women's problems and illnesses – from the Greek *gynaikos*, 'woman', and *logos*, 'the study of something'.

Gynaecomastia

Man breasts – from the Greek *gynaikos*, 'woman', and *mastos*, 'breast'. This is a condition which affects fifty per cent of men over the age of fifty and seems to be becoming more common in younger men. It is the phenomenon of 'man breasts', excessive development of the male breast tissue. There are theories (unproven) that it is to do with the increasing use of chemicals in general and the possibility of artificial female hormones passing into the water cycle and thence being consumed by men to trigger breast development.

H

Habenda ratio valetudinis
'We must pay attention to our health.' Motto of the Royal Pharmaceutical Society.

Habet natura, ut aliarum omnium rerum, sic vivendi modum
'Nature prescribes moderation in living as in all things' – Cicero. A maxim that is as true today as it was in the first century, when Marcus Tullius Cicero wrote it. See *Cicero*. c.f. *Modus omnibus in rebus optimum est habitu*.

Hac nocte
'Tonight.' In prescription-writing the abbreviation *hac.noc.* could be used when something has to be taken on the night of the prescription.

Haec olim meminisse juvabit
'Time heals all wounds.'

Haematemesis
Vomiting of blood – from the Greek *haema* or *haimatos*, 'blood', and *emesis*, 'vomiting'.

Haemorrhage
Blood loss – from the Greek words *haima*, 'blood', and *rrhagia*, 'gushing out'.

Halitosis
Bad breath – from the Latin, *halitus*, 'breath', and the Greek *osis*, meaning 'abnormal condition of'.

Hallucination
A false perception, visual or auditory – from the Latin *alucinari*, 'mind-wandering'.

Hallux
The big toe – from the Latin word *(h)allex*, meaning 'big toe'.

Hallux rigidus
Stiff big toe. Sometimes this is also described as *hallux flexus, hallux limitus, metatarsus primus elevatus*, or *hallux dolorosus*. They all refer to a stiff hammer-toe deformity of the big toe. It is the second commonest condition affecting this digit.

Hallux valgus
An inward pointing big toe. This is usually, but not always, due to a bunion.

Harvey, William
William Harvey (1578–1657) was born in Folkestone, England, and educated at the King's School, Canterbury, then at Gonville and Caius College, Cambridge, from which he received a BA in 1597. From there he went to study under the anatomist Fabricius at the University of Padua, from whence he graduated in 1602. He returned to England and married Elizabeth Brown, daughter of the court physician to Elizabeth I. In time he became court physician to King Charles I. After much research on animals he demonstrated the circulation of the blood

and announced his discovery of the circulatory system in 1616. In 1628 he published his work *Exercitatio Anatomica de Motu Cordis et Sanguinis in Animalibus (An Anatomical Exercise on the Motion of the Heart and Blood in Animals)*. It was the most significant piece of medical research ever written and laid the foundation for the scientific study of medicine.

Haustus
'A draught.' In prescription-writing the abbreviation *haust.* could be used when a draught is to be dispensed.

Hepatitis
Inflammation of the liver – from the Greek words *hepatos*, meaning 'liver' and *itis*, 'inflammation'.

Hepatomegaly
Enlargement of the liver, from whatever cause – from the Greek words, *hepatos*, 'liver', and *megale*, meaning 'enlargement'.

Hereditas domini filii
'Children are a heritage from the Lord.' Motto of the Royal College of Paediatrics and Child Health.

Hernia
From the Latin word, *hernia*, meaning 'a rupture'. It usually refers to the bursting of an organ, as the result of trauma, or the protrusion of an organ or tissues through a breach in the muscles.

Hiatus hernia
A hernia of the stomach through the diaphragm – from the Latin words, *hiatus*, meaning 'opening', and *hernia*,

'rupture'. This condition means that part of the stomach protrudes through the diaphragm into the thorax. As a result, the valve-like action at the top of the stomach is lost and acid may be allowed to squirt into the oesophagus (gullet), thereby producing the symptom of heartburn.

Herpes

A viral infection caused by one or other of the viruses in the *herpes* group. The word comes from the Greek *herpein*, to creep. The condition tends to creep up and spread insidiously.

Herpes simplex – this causes cold sores and blistering eruptions on the face, the eye and the skin. When it causes cold sores on the mouth it is called *Herpes labialis* (from the Latin *labialis*, referring to lips). A variant also causes *Herpes genitalis*, a blistering, painful condition affecting the genitals. *Herpes zoster* (from the Greek *zoster*, meaning girdle) is the virus that causes chickenpox and shingles. Shingles occurs when the virus, which remains dormant in a skin nerve, suddenly becomes active. It produces painful eruptions in the skin distribution of that nerve. It is usually one-sided and so painful that it used to be called the devil's rosary.

Hippocrates of Cos

Hippocrates of Cos (circa 460 BCE–380 BCE) was an Ancient Greek physician, commonly regarded as 'the father of medicine'. He was a physician from the so-called medical school of Cos. Writings attributed to him (the *Corpus Hippocraticum*, or Hippocratic Writings) rejected the superstition and magic of earlier medicine and laid the foundations of medicine as a noble and scientific profession.

Hippocratic Oath

The Hippocratic Oath is one of the most popular selections of ancient literature, even though the original oath is rarely read or recited. For several centuries now, modified versions of the oath, containing the essence of its message, have been taken by doctors upon qualification. The original oath was almost certainly not written by Hippocrates himself but the work is traditionally included in the *Corpus Hippocraticum*, a collection of medical writings attributed to him, written between the fifth and fourth centuries BCE. The Oath originally written in Greek begins: 'I swear by Apollo the physician, and Asclepius, and Hygieia, and Panacea, and all the gods and goddesses, that, according to my ability and judgement, I will keep this Oath and this stipulation....' Asclepius (Aesculapius to the Romans) was the Greek god of healing, and Hygieia and Panacea were his two daughters. It is said that Aesculapius always preferred Hygieia (hygiene). See *hygiene* and *panacea*.

Hirudo

'A leach.' Leaches used to be prescribed commonly and are making a comeback into medicine and surgery thanks to their incredible ability to reduce bruising.

Homo

'Man.' Scientifically, this refers to any primate of the genus *Homo*, including modern man and the extinct, so-called missing links.

Homoeopathy

A system of therapeutics for treating people and animals on the basis of the *simile principle.* The word 'homoeopathy' was coined by Dr Samuel Hahnemann

(1755–1843) from the Greek words *homoios*, meaning similar or like and *pathos*, meaning suffering. Essentially, this means that it is a therapeutic method using preparations of substances whose effects, when administered to healthy subjects, correspond to the manifestations of the disorder (the symptoms, clinical signs and pathological states) in the patient. It is a system that is practised across the world. Most of the remedies, of which there are in excess of 4,000, are referred to by their Latin names. Critics of homoeopathy have difficulty with the dilute states of the remedies used, believing that this dilution is the defining characteristic of the method. It is not, because the defining characteristic is the simile principle, as explained above. The individual's experience of the condition is of paramount importance, and the indicated treatment is the remedy that most closely matches the profile of patients' experience of their illness. See *similia similibus curentur* and *contraria contrariis curantur*.

Homoeostasis

The internal balance of the body – from the Greek *homoios*, 'similar', or 'like', and *stasis*, 'stillness'. This refers to the body's internal mechanisms that automatically maintain balance of organs and systems. For example, blood sugar levels, blood pressure, temperature control.

Homo sapiens

'Wise man.' This is the name for the human species, as originated by Linnaeus. See *Linnaeus*.

Honoris causa

'For honour's sake.' Honorary degrees (e.g. *doctora honoris causa)* are awarded *honoris causa*. The abbreviation *h.c.* is added after the degree, hence Doctor of Science, DSc, h.c.

Horace

Quintus Horatius Flaccus (65 BCE–8 BCE) was a Latin poet famous for his four books of odes (known in Latin as *Carmina*), which contain over one hundred individual poems. In one of these odes Horace bragged that his poetry would live as long as Vestal Virgins climbed the Capitoline Hill in Rome. Interestingly, there are no longer any Vestal Virgins in modern Rome, but Horace's odes are still going strong! The odes cover all sorts things from dinner invitations to philosophical musings and pieces in praise of the good life. Many of his Latin phrases are still in use today, such as *carpe diem*, 'seize the day', and *aurea mediocritas*, the 'golden mean'.

Hora somni

'At the hour of sleep.' In prescription-writing *h.s* means to take a medicine before going to sleep. This could also be written as *Hora somni surendus*, to be taken at bedtime, abbreviated to *h.s.s.*

Hordeolum

A stye – from *hordeolum*, 'grain of barley'. A stye is a painful infected swelling of a tiny gland on the eyelid rim. It is called thus because of its resemblance to a grain of barley.

Humor

Vital fluid of the body – from the Latin *umor* or *humor*, meaning 'moisture or fluid'. Until the Renaissance the dominant philosophy in medicine was based upon the Doctrine of Humors or the Humoral Theory of disease. It was believed that the balance between four vital fluids governed the state of health or disease within the body. The concept is still adhered to in Unani, a traditional form of medicine widely practised in India and Sri Lanka. In anatomy we still use the term in relation to body fluids like bile and lymph and to the two fluids of the eye, the *aqueus humor* in the chamber in front of the lens, and the *vitreous humor* in the posterior chamber behind the lens. See *Doctrine of Humors*.

Humanum est errare
To err is human.

Humerus
Upper arm bone – from the Latin, *humerus*. The largest bone of the arm. The head of the humerus fits into the glenoid cavity of the scapula (shoulder blade). At its lower end is the olecranon fossa, into which the olecranon (elbow point) fits as a hinge joint. The humerus is sometimes called the 'funny bone', partly because its name is misinterpreted as humorous and partly because when the elbow is knocked it produces a painful numbness for a few moments. This is due to the fact that the ulnar nerve is partly exposed as it crosses the inside of the elbow, and a blow to it produces numbness in the area that it supplies. See *olecranon*.

Hunter, John
John Hunter (1728–93) was a Scottish surgeon regarded as one of the most distinguished scientists of his day. He was born near East Kilbride in Scotland, the youngest of ten children. He studied under his brother, William Hunter, who owned his own School of Anatomy in London. After qualifying he was commissioned as an

Army surgeon in 1760 and spent three years in France and Portugal. Apart from his surgical discoveries, he made extensive anatomical dissections of numerous species and of convicted felons. In 1767 he was elected as Fellow of the Royal Society and in 1768 he was appointed Surgeon to St George's Hospital in London. Later he became a member of the Company of Surgeons. In 1776 he was appointed surgeon to King George III. He left a collection of nearly 14,000 preparations of over 500 species of plants and animals. Much of the collection can still be seen in the Hunterian Museum of the Royal College of Surgeons of London.

Hydronephrosis
Swelling of the kidney – literally, water on the kidney. From the Greek *hydros*, 'water' and the Greek, *nephros*, 'kidney'. This is usually caused by a back pressure on the kidney, from a stone, or other obstruction of flow in the urinary tract.

Hydrops
An unnatural collection of fluid in any cavity of the body – from the Latin *hydropsis*, meaning, 'from water'. The condition of gross hydrops, or gross oedema, swelling of the legs, most usually due to heart, liver or kidney failure, has been recognized since antiquity. The Romans also called it *aquosis languor*, because of the tiredness and lethargy that accompany the swelling. It time it became known as dropsy, an abbreviated version of Hydrops. There is a reference to it in the Bible (Good News Bible). In Luke 14: 1–6, Jesus treats a man whose legs and arms were swollen. In 1775, Dr William Withering was making a journey from his home in Birmingham to see patients at Stafford Infirmary. While the horses were being

changed on his carriage he was asked to see an old lady with dropsy. He pronounced her incurable and went on his way to see his other patients. Some weeks later he heard of her recovery and enquired as to how it had occurred. He discovered that she had been drinking a herbal tea made up of about twenty herbs. Withering perceived that the active ingredient was the foxglove – *Digitalis purpurea*. Research over ten years resulted in the publication of *An Account of the Foxglove and some of its Medical Uses* in 1785, which contained reports on clinical trials and notes on digitalis toxicity. It was the discovery of a drug that (in synthetic form) is still used today and has transformed the lives of many heart patients. See also *endolymphatic hydrops*.

Hydrophobia
The old name for rabies – from the Greek *hydros*, 'water' and *phobos*, 'fear'. This is a highly dangerous viral disease that affects the brain and central nervous system, after being bitten by a rabid animal. In the later stages of the disease there is abnormal behaviour, increased salivation, dehydration and painful spasms of the throat. Hence the idea that there is fear of swallowing water. See *rabies*.

Hydrops gravidarum
Tissue swelling due to fluid retention in pregnancy.

Hygiene
The promotion of good health, especially by maintaining scrupulous cleanliness. It comes from the name of the Greek goddess, Hygieia the goddess of health. Hygieia was the daughter of Asclepius and the sister of Panacea. While her father and sister were connected with the treatment of disease Hygieia was regarded as being

concerned with the preservation of good health and the prevention of disease. It is supposedly for this reason that Asclepius favoured Hygieia.

Hymen
The membrane partially covering the vaginal opening – from the Greek *hymen*, meaning 'membrane'. This name comes from Greek mythology, Hymen being the god of weddings. In days gone by an intact hymen was considered evidence of maidenhood, or virginity, hence it was called the maidenhead. In fact, few females reach marriage with an intact hymen, or *virgo intacta*, not because of having had intercourse but simply because it is a fragile membrane that can be damaged by vigorous exercise, petting or masturbation.

Hyperemesis gravidarum
Excessive sickness in pregnancy. This is more serious than *nausea gravidarum*, the usual pregnancy sickness that most expectant mothers experience. It can be so severe as to affect the mother's acid-base balance and may require hospitalization and medical treatment.

Hypertension
High blood pressure – from the Greek *hyper*, 'excessive', and the Latin *tensionis*, meaning 'stretched out'.

Hyperthyroidism
Overactivity of the thyroid gland – from the Greek words *hyper*, excessive and *thyreo-eides*, a notched shield as used by Ancient Greek foot soldiers. The thyroid gland controls the metabolism of the body. Excess activity results in hyperthyroidism, which used to be called Graves' disease. The patient with this condition usually

loses weight, may experience racing of the heart, and may become aware of a slight protuberance of the eyeballs – exophthalmos. See *exophthalmos*.

Hypertrophy
Excessive growth of tissue – from the Greek *hyper*, 'excessive' and *trophe*, 'nourishment'. This rather implies that if you overfeed a tissue it will enlarge. This is not strictly the case. Hypertrophy is a process of enlargement of tissue, which may be physiological (and good) or pathological (and bad).

Hypnosis
The process of inducing a sleep-like trance – from the Greek *hypnos*, 'sleep' and *osis*, 'abnormal condition'. Hypnotherapy is the use of the hypnotic trance in a therapeutic manner.

Hypnotic
A drug that induces sleep. A sleeping tablet in other words. Hypnos was the Greek god of sleep.

Hypo– conditions
Deficiency states or underactivity conditions. For example, *hypoglycaemia* means 'low blood sugar', *hypothyroidism* means 'an underactive thyroid condition' and *hypovitaminosis* means 'a deficiency of vitamins'.

Hypodermic
Under the skin – from the Greek *hypo*, 'under', and *dermatos*, 'skin'. In common speech this is taken to mean a hypodermic syringe.

I

Iatrogenic illness

Doctor-made illness – from the Greek *iatros*, 'doctor', and the Greek *gen*, 'made by'. Iatrogenic illness occurs frequently as a result of the drugs or treatments that are given. This is a recognized problem, accounting for up to ten per cent of all hospitalizations.

Icthyosis

The term ichthyosis comes from the Greek *ichthys*, meaning 'fish', and refers to the clinical appearance of scaly skin .

Id

It – from *id*, meaning 'it'. The Id, according to Sigmund Freud, constitutes part of one's unconscious mind. It is organized around primitive instinctual urges of sexuality, aggression and the desire for instant gratification or release. See *Ego and Superego* and *Freud*.

Id est

'That is, that means.' This is used frequently to explain points in texts and papers. It is usually abbreviated to *i.e.*

Idiopathic

Disease of the individual – from the Greek *idios*, 'of an individual' and the Greek *pathos*, 'suffering or disease'. An idiopathic illness is something that seems to affect an individual but without any obvious cause. Although there is a cause, it just evades medical knowledge at the moment.

Idiosyncrasy

Something (a reaction of some sort) that is unique to the individual – from the Greek *idios*, 'of an individual', and the Greek *syn*, 'together', and the Greek *krasis*, 'mix'. An idiosyncratic reaction is a unique effect or reaction to a food or treatment that does not tend to cause a problem.

Ientaculum

'At breakfast.' See *jentaculum*.

Ignis sacer

Literally, 'holy fire'. This refers to St Anthony's Fire, a mysterious epidemic illness associated with huge blistering eruptions, gangrene of the digits or limbs, hallucinations, mania, psychosis and death, that occurred in Antiquity and well into the Middle Ages. It is now known that this was due to ergotism, caused by eating rye contaminated by a fungus. Virgil and Pliny the Elder were both aware of these epidemics. Undoubtedly, isolated cases of other conditions like erysipelas and gas gangrene would have occurred and would have been confused with it. The earliest reference to it comes from the *Annales Xantenses* for the year 857: 'a great plague of swollen blisters consumed the people by a loathsome rot, so that their limbs were loosened and fell off before death.' In medieval times it was known as *ignis sacer* (holy fire or St Anthony's Fire), after the fourth-century hermit of Egypt. The order of St Anthony was formed to look after victims of this condition. It is believed that the women accused of witchcraft in the Salem trials of 1692 were suffering from ergot-induced psychosis and convulsions. Ergot derivatives have been used for many years in the treatment of migraine.

Ileostomy
An operation to make an opening in the ileum, and bring it out on to the abdominal wall. This may be done when the whole of the colon is being removed.

Ileum
The longest part of the small intestine, between the jejunum and the large bowel, the colon – from the Greek *eilos*, 'twisted'. A look inside the abdomen gives you the impression that this part of the intestine is a mass of twisted loops.

Ilium
The large bone on each side of the sacrum, which helps to make a basin shape of the pelvis (Latin *pelvis*, 'basin'). The word is derived from the Latin *ilia*, 'flanks'.

Immedicabile vulnus
'An incurable wound' – Ovid, *Metamorphoses*, 1, 190. See *Ovid*.

In articulo mortis
'At the point of death'. Cf. *In extremis*.

Incus
Ear anvil – from *incus*, 'anvil'. One of the ossicles in the middle ear. See *ossicles*.

In extremis
'At the point of death.' cf *In articulo mortis*.

Inferior
Lower – from the Latin *inferior*, 'lower'. This is a useful anatomical term, which tells how one structure relates to another.

Infra
'Under, below.'

Inhalatio
'An inhalation.' In prescription-writing the abbreviation *inhal.* could be used when an inhalation was to be dispensed.

In loco parentis
'In the place or in the position of a parent.' An institution or hospital may find itself in this situation.

In morbo recolligit se animus
'In sickness the mind reflects upon itself' – Pliny, Book 7. See *Pliny the Elder*.

In morbus minus
'Less of everything in disease' – Hippocrates. See *Hippocrates*.

In naturalibus
'Naked'.

In situ
'In its natural place.' An organ is *in situ* when it is in its correct anatomical position and has not been operated upon. A pathological process can sometimes be *in situ*, which means that it is in a very early stage.

Insomnia
Inability to sleep – from *insomnis*, 'sleepless'.

In somno securitas
'Safe in sleep.' Motto of the Association of Anaesthetists of Great Britain and Ireland. It is to be hoped so – your life is literally in their hands.

Instillandus
'To be dropped in.' In prescription-writing the abbreviation *instill.* could be used when something has to be dropped into another liquid.

Insulin
The hormone that controls sugar levels within the body – from *insula*, 'an island'. Insulin is secreted from the islets of Langerhans in the pancreas.

Intemperans adolescentia effectum corpus tradit senectuti
'An intemperate youth brings to old age a worn out body' – Cicero, *De Senectute*, 9, 20. See *Cicero*.

Inter-
'Between.' Thus *intervertebral* discs are the discs between vertebrae. *Interossei* are the muscles between bones.

Interossei
'Between bones.' There are seven interossei muscles between the metatarsal bones of each foot and the metacarpal bones of each hand. There are four on the back and three on the front of each hand and foot.

Intestine
The digestive tract from the duodenum to the rectum – from *intestinus*, 'guts'.

Intra
'Within.'

Intradermal
'Into the dermis.' In prescription-writing the abbreviation *ID*, could be used when an injection is to be made into the dermis layer of the skin.

Intra mural
'Within the wall.' This can be used to describe a lesion in the wall of a particular organ.

Intramuscular
'Into the muscles.' In prescription-writing the abbreviation *IM*, could be used when an injection is to be made into the muscles, usually of the arm, buttock or the thigh.

Intravenous
'Into a vein.' In prescription-writing the abbreviation *IV*, could be used when an injection is to be made directly into a vein.

In utero
'Within the uterus or womb.' It can be used to describe something as being actually within the uterus, such as an intrauterine contraceptive device (IUCD) – a coil. And it can be used to talk about the developing baby within the womb.

In vitro
'In the test tube.' Hence, in vitro fertilisation (IVF), or 'test-tube babies.'

In vivo
'In the living state.'

Involution
The old name for the menopause – from *involvere*, 'the process of enfolding', 'returning'. In the context of the womb it is a returning to an infertile stage. It was thought that at a certain age the womb would shrivel and enfold or go back to pre-fertile days. This was also thought to result in the mood changes of depression.

Involutional melancholia
The old name for depression at the menopause – from *involvere*, 'the process of enfolding or returning', and 'melancholia'. See *melancholia*.

Ischium
The rump bone – from the Greek *ischio*, 'rump'. The lowest part of the pelvis is composed of the two ischia bones. The big gluteal muscles give shape to the bottom, but in the process of sitting down they slide over the ischia, to leave them less well padded than they are when you stand up. That is unfortunate because when you have been sitting too long you may become aware that you have been sitting on your bones. And you have been, literally. Of course, some people have more prominent ischial spines, or bonier bottoms, than others. They may envy those with bonnier bottoms than themselves.

J

Jejunum
Empty – from *jejunus*, 'empty'. The jejunum follows on from the duodenum and joins on to the small intestine. The Greek physician and anatomist Galen described it as empty, because he believed that it was always found to be empty after death.

Jejunus raro stomachus vulgaria temnit
The hungry stomach rarely despises common food – Horace. See *Horace*.

Jentaculum
'At breakfast.' In prescription-writing the abbreviation *jentac.* could be used when something was to be taken with breakfast. See *Ientaculum*.

Jugular vein
The vein of the throat – from *jugulum*, 'throat' and *vena*, 'vein'. There is an internal and an external jugular vein on each side of the throat. It is one of the main veins returning blood towards the heart from the head and neck. There is no jugular artery, which will be bad news, not to mention a surprise, to many writers of crime novels.

Juvenal
Decimus Iunius Iuvenalis, was a Roman satiric poet of the first century. He was born at Aquinum in Italy. His

writing focused on the corruption of Roman society. He is known for coining the phrase *panem et circenses* ('bread and circuses'), which he described as the prime pursuits of the Roman populace. He wrote the *Satirae (Satires).*

K

Keloid

Overscarring – from the Greek *kele*, 'tumour' and the Greek *eides*, 'form'. Keloid is overscarring, as the tissues overheal. It can be a problem for people having surgery, because even a very fine incision may overheal to produce an excessively large scar.

Keratin

The horny tissues of the nails and the skin – from the Greek *keras*, 'horn'.

Keratosis

Disorder of the horny tissue – from the Greek *keras* and *osis*, 'disorder of'. Typically, this occurs in the skin as *solar keratoses*, often called liver spots and seborrhoeic warts.

Kyphosis

Stooped posture – from the Greek *kyphos*, 'stoop' and the Greek *–osis*, 'condition'. This is the round-backed appearance that occurs in the elderly with osteoporosis, or other conditions that cause the spine to bend forward. Richard III, a famous hunchback, had a kyphosis.

L

Labia

Lip – from *labium*, 'lip'. The oral labii (plural of labium) consist of fleshy tissue surrounding the main muscle of the lips, the *orbicularis oris*, the sphincter muscle of the mouth. The female labii of the perineum, consist of the outer lips, the larger *labii majora* (plural of *labium majus*) and the smaller inner lips, the *labii minora* (plural of *Labium minus*). Under the apex of the labii minora is the clitoris. See *clitoris*, *orbicularis oris*, and *sphincter*.

Laboratory

The 'science work room' – from *laboratorium*, itself from *laborare*, 'to work'. Modern medicine leans heavily upon the pathology laboratory and the various sciences that are practised in them. The 'path lab' is usually divided into various departments which cover the various disciplines. The haematology department test the blood, the bone marrow and the clotting ability of the blood. The medical biochemistry department test the blood for various enzymes, electrolytes and specific compounds in the management of a myriad of medical conditions. The microbiological department test body fluids and samples in order to determine the nature of infections and to pinpoint the appropriate antibiotics that should be used to combat them.

Labyrinth
The labyrinth is a system of fluid passages in the inner ear, consisting of the vestibular system (balance sytem) and the auditory sytem. It is a complex structure that takes its name from the maze of Greek mythology, *labyrinthos*, through which the Minotaur roamed. In the legend Theseus used a reel of thread to find his way out of the labyrinth.

Lac
Milk. In prescription-writing the abbreviation *lac.* indicates milk, or a particular type of milk. In days gone by, placebo tablets were prescribed containing nothing other than milk sugar, *Saccharum Lactis*. In homoeopathic medicine many *lac* or milk remedies are still used – *Lac caninum* (dog's milk), *Lac defloratum* (skimmed milk), *Lac felinum* (cat's milk), *Lac vaccinum* (cow's milk).

Lacrima
Tear – from *lacrima*, meaning 'tear'.

Lacrimal duct
The tear duct – from *lacrimalis*, 'of the tears' and *ductus*, 'canal'. See *dacryocystitis*.

Laparotomy
To open the abdomen – from *lapara*, 'loins' and *otomy*, 'to open'. A laparotomy is the operation to open the abdomen to perform a surgical procedure on an organ.

Lapsus calami
'Slip of the pen, misprint'.

Lapsus linguae
'Slip of the tongue.' Freud would consider that a slip of the tongue is not the accidental misuse of one word for another but represents an association that is lurking under the surface in the unconscious mind. The so-called Freudian slip usually has a sexual connotation. See *Freud*.

Lapsus memoriae
'Lapse of memory.'

Latent
Something that is present, but not yet active – from Latin *latens*, derived from *latere*, 'to lie hidden'. In medicine something is latent when it is dormant, smouldering away. An infection can be latent.

Latent fingerprint
In forensic medicine, a fingerprint made by deposits of oils and/or perspiration, not usually visible to the human eye. Various technologies, including lasers, can be used to identify latent prints.

Lateral
The side – from *lateralis*, 'of the side'.

Lateri dolente
'To the affected (painful) side.' In prescription-writing the abbreviation *lat. dol.* could be used when something, usually a lotion or embrocation, was to be applied to the painful side.

Latine dictum
'Spoken in Latin.'

Latine scriptum

'Written in Latin.' Most prescriptions are written in English (or the language of the prescriber) although some of the prescribing terms are still Latin abbreviations. See, for example, *ad lib, agita, ante cibos, ante meridiem, auris dextra, auris sinistra, bis in die, occulus dexter, occulus sinistra, post cibos, quaque die, quaque horis, quater in die, pro re nata, sub lingua, ter in die.*

Latissimus dorsi

The broad muscle of the back – from *latissimo*, derived from *latus*, meaning 'broad' and *dorsum*, 'the back'. The latissimus dorsi muscle in the back is attached to the pelvic girdle and vertebral column and is inserted into the midline of the humerus (upper arm bone). Body-builders refer to their 'lats'. It functions to pull the arm toward the back as in rowing a boat or in a swimming motion.

Lens

The lens of the eye – from the Latin *lens*, meaning 'lentil'. This curious origin relates to the shape of the eye lens, on account of its resemblance to the seed of a lentil.

Leprosy

This is an ancient illness caused by a bacillus, *Mycobacterium leprae*, which multiplies very slowly and mainly affects the skin, nerves, and mucous membranes. The name comes from the Late Latin word, *lepra*. Leprosy was recognized by the ancient civilizations of Egypt, China and India, and was first written about as far back as the sixth century BCE. In days gone by, people suffering from this disease were considered outcasts and had to live on their own outside their communities, or were sent to leper colonies to die slowly of their disease. Fortunately, nowadays it is curable and deformities are preventable if treatment is started early.

Levator muscles
Lifting muscles – from *levare*, 'to lift'. There are several muscles whose function is to lift a structure to which they are attached. For example:

Levator anguli oris – which pulls the corner of the lip up in an almost vertical direction, sharply angling the lip corners up in a supercilious smile. It is also called the caninus muscle.

Levator ani – this is a sling of muscle that surrounds the rectum and acts as a sort of internal valve. When one opens one's bowels, the muscle relaxes so that the rectum straightens and a motion can be easily passed.

Levator palpebrae superiorus – the upper eyelid muscle.

Ligate
To tie something off – from *ligare*, 'to tie, bind'. Commonly, a surgeon will ligate a bleeding vessel during an operation with some sort of suture material.

Linctus
A soothing cough remedy – from *lingere*, *linctum*, 'to lick and soothe'. In prescription-writing the abbreviation *linct.* would be used when a linctus is to be dispensed.

Linimentum
'A liniment.' In prescription-writing the abbreviation *lin.* would be used when a liniment is to be dispensed.

Linnaeus

Carolus Linnaeus (1707–78) is the Latinized version of Carl von Linne, the Swedish botanist whose systems of classification and nomenclature had a revolutionary effect on the study of all living things. Having originally intended to become a doctor, he instead turned his attention to botany. His classification system developed during the time that he was restoring the famous botanical garden at Uppsala University and became the basis for almost all subsequent systems of biological nomenclature. The Linnaean system classified living things within a hierarchy, starting with two kingdoms – plants and animals. Kingdoms were divided into classes and they, in turn, were subdivided into orders, families, genera (singular: genus), and species (singular: species). Other ranks have been added since then but the basic classification was laid down by Linnaeus. The crux of the system was that you could describe any organism with a binomial or two-word description, consisting of the generic (genus) name and the specific (species) name. Thus, he was the first to describe human beings as *Homo sapiens* (wise man). Bacteria are classified by the same genus and species names, for example *Escherichia coli*, and *Streptococcus viridans*. By convention their names are usually italicized. See *bacteria*.

Livid

Angry or bruised looking – from *lividus*, 'blue-black look'. In common parlance someone is livid with rage. In medicine it means bruised looking, or perhaps inflamed.

Livor mortis

'Bruising after death'. Lividity, or bruised discoloration after death, comes about because the dark, deoxygenated blood stagnates in dependent parts of the body. Hence, depth of lividity and the places where it occurs may give some idea as to the timing of death.

Livy

Titus Livius (circa 64 BCE–AD 17) was born in Patavium (modern day Padua) in north-eastern Italy. Together with Sallust and Tacitus, he was one of the three great Roman historians. He wrote a monumental history of Rome from its founding in 753 BCE, entitled *Ab Urbe Condita (From the Founding of the City* – Roman dates started with 1 ABC – *ab urbe condita*). Written in chronological order, with a narrative style, it became a classic in his own lifetime and acted as a blueprint for historical texts down to the eighteenth century.

Locum tenens

'Holding the place.' A *locum tenens* is a deputy. When a doctor is on holiday, a *locum tenens* is employed to take his or her place.

Lotis (or lautis) minibus

'With clean hands.'

Lucretius

Titus Lucretius Carus (99 BCE–55 BCE) was a Roman poet and proto-scientist and the author of the philosophical epic *De Rerum Natura (On the Nature of the Universe)*, in which he expounded on the Epicurean philosophy. In this philosophy one can see the blueprint for Western science. His epic six volumes give an explanation of the physical origin, structure, and destiny of the universe, all based upon the nature of atoms.

Lumbago
Low back pain, from *lumbago*, 'loin pain'.

Lumbar
The lower back or loin – from *lumbus*, 'loin'. A lumbar puncture (LP) is a procedure to remove cerebrospinal fluid for analysis in cases of possible infection or inflammation.

Lumbricales
'Worm muscles' – from the Latin *lumbricus*, 'an earthworm'. There are four small worm-like muscles in the hand, which pass into the four fingers. They help to flex the fingers, as when giving a cute wave by flapping the fingers at an angle to the palm. One of my old anatomy teachers used to end his tutorials by smiling cruelly and waving like this, as he whispered, 'see you at the re-sit exams!' The worm!

Lumen
An opening – from *lumen*, 'light'. A lumen refers to the channel through which air or blood flows. You can talk about the lumen of a hollow organ or the lumen of a blood vessel. A thrombosis refers to the blockage of the lumen of a blood vessel by a blood clot.

Lusus naturae
'A freak of nature.'

M

Macrobius
Ambrosius Theodosius Macrobius, (AD 395–AD 423) was a Roman writer and philosopher. His *Saturnalia*, a dialogue in seven books chiefly concerned with a literary evaluation of Virgil, incorporates valuable quotations from other writers. The seventh book mainly deals with physiology.

Malaria
An infectious disease, originally called swamp fever – from *malus aria*, 'bad air'. Malaria is the world's most important infectious tropical disease, affecting more than a hundred million people each year, and resulting in over a million deaths a year. It was originally thought that it was due to bad air, from the vapours rising from swamps. We now know that this feverish illness is due to an infection with one of four species of Plasmodium, a protozoan (one-celled) parasite that invades the red blood cells and the liver and spleen. It is spread by the bite of an infected female anopheles mosquito. It causes cycles of fever, chills, joint pains, vomiting and at its worst, coma and death. Classically, these 'chill-and-fever' episodes (paroxysms) occur when the parasites are released from the red blood cells. This happens periodically to produce different patterns of fever. For examples, the paroxysms associated with a tertian malaria (e.g. *Plasmodium vivax*) occur about every forty-eight hours, and those associated

with a quartan malaria (e.g. *Plasmodium malariae*) occur about every seventy-two hours. See *fever*.

Male secum agit aeger, medicum qui haeredem facit
'A sick man does ill for himself who makes the doctor his heir' – Publilius Syrus. See *Syrus, Publilius*.

Malignant
Growing worse – from *malignans*, the Latin for 'growing worse'. In pathology a malignant condition usually (but not always) refers to a cancerous condition. Left to itself it will undoubtedly grow worse, so it requires swift and usually powerful measures. c.f. *benign*.

Malleolus
Little hammer – from *malleus*, 'hammer' *oleus*, and 'smaller'. The malleoli (plural of malleolus) are the bony protrusions on each side of the ankles. The protrusion of the fibula is the outer, external or lateral malleolus, and the protrusion of the tibia is the inner, or medial malleolus.

Malleus
Ear hammer – from *malleus*, 'hammer'. One of the ossicles in the middle ear. See *ossicles*.

Mammary glands, mammae
The breasts – from the Latin *mamma*, 'breast'.

Mandible
The lower jaw – from the Late Latin *mandibulum*, derived from *mandere*, 'to chew' – hence literally 'little chewer'.

Mane
'In the morning.' In prescription-writing *mane*. is written when something is to be taken in the morning.

Mane et vespere

'Morning and evening.' In prescription-writing the abbreviation *M. et V.* would be used if a drug was to be taken in the morning and repeated in the evening.

Mane primo

'Early in the morning.' In prescription-writing the abbreviation *M.P.* or *man.prim.* would be used when something is to be taken first thing in the morning, before breakfast. c.f. *prima luce.*

Mania

'Rage, madness' – from Late Latin *mania*, itself derived from the Greek. The term is not much used these days. Manic-depressive psychosis, in which the individual may flit from an acute, sometimes elated, sometimes angry state with poor insight, into a state of utter depression, is now diagnosed as bipolar disorder. The old term had a pejorative meaning that no longer has a place in modern medicine.

Maniae infinitae sunt species

'The different sorts of madness are infinite' – Avicenna. See *Avicenna.*

Manilius

Marcus Manilius was a Roman poet, astrologer, and author of a poem in five books called *Astronomica*. He flourished in the first century. His writing gives us a good insight into the beliefs of the Romans, and into their dependence upon the study of astrology in all areas of life.

Martial

Marcus Valerius Martialis, known as Martial (AD 40– AD 103) was a Latin poet and military tribune. In AD 80,

Martial published *Liber Spectaculorum (On the Spectacles)*, in celebration of the Colosseum. He followed this with more undistinguished epigrams and then between AD 86 and 102 he wrote the twelve books of epigrams on which his fame is based. He is considered to be the creator of the modern epigram. He depicted Roman life through the medium of these epigrams, many of which are colourful to say the least.

Masseter
The large chewing muscle – from the Greek, *maseter*, 'a chewer'. This large muscle is the main closing muscle of the lower jaw. It was described by the Greek physician Galen. It is the muscle that stands out when you grit your teeth, as all readers of romantic fiction will be aware. A couple of good rippling Masseter muscles indicate 'hero' (or greedy-chops). See *Galen*.

Mastoid bone
The small lump behind the ear, which contains the mastoid antrum, a space that is in connection with the middle ear. It is so named because it is a small hump that resembles a female breast, from the Greek *mastos*, 'breast' and the Greek *eides*, 'form or like'.

Masturbate
To stimulate oneself sexually – from *mas*, 'male' and *turbare*, 'to agitate'. Clearly in days gone-by masturbation was considered solely a male act, or rather, it was assumed that only males did it. We now know that the majority of people of both sexes masturbate at various times, and no one should feel guilty about it. It is normal and will not be followed by any of the awesome and

terrible illnesses that Victorian fathers promised would befall their wayward children.

Materia medica
'Medical material.' This has come to mean the pharmacology of drugs. In homoeopathic medicine the *Materia Medica* is the listing of all of the homoeopathic remedies, with their indications, profiles, sources, etc. By convention homoeopathic remedies are called by their Latin names. Some of the commonly used remedes are: *Arsenicum album, Baryta carbonica, natrum muriaticum, Ranunculus bulbosus, Thuja occidentalis* and *Zincum metallicum.*

Mature fiera senem, si diu velis esse senex
'You must become an old man in good time if you wish to be an old man long' – Cicero, *De Senecute,* 10. See *Cicero.*

Maxilla
The upper jaw – from *mala,* 'jaw'.

Medice, cura te ipsum
'Physician, heal thyself.' This well known phrase comes from Luke 4: 23 in the Vulgate Bible. Every doctor who has had the temerity to come down with a cold will have been the butt of this witticism. Yet there is a serious point, which applies to people other than doctors: if you give advice, you should heed it yourself. See *Vulgate.*

Medici causa morbid inventa, curationem esse inventam putant
'Physicians, when the cause of disease is discovered, consider that the cure is discovered' – Cicero, *Tusc, Quest.* If only it were as simple as that! See *Cicero.*

Medicinae Baccalaureus – Baccalaureus Chirurgia

Bachelor of Medicine, Bachelor of Surgery. Bachelor of Medicine is usually abbreviated to MB or BM, and Bachelor of Surgery is abbreviated to ChB, BCh or BS. They are awarded as a conjoint degree in British medical schools and many other countries around the world as the first qualifying degree. Thus MB, ChB, or MB, BCh, or BM, BS. Holders are permitted to use the title 'doctor'. See *Medicinae Doctoris*.

Medicinae Doctoris

Doctor of Medicine. In the United States the standard qualifying medical degree is MD, which is the equivalent of MB, ChB. In the United Kingdom and many other countries an MD is a second, postgraduate degree, conferred after a period of research and a doctoral thesis. See *Medicinae Baccalaureus – Baccalaureus Chirurgia*.

Medicina mortuorum sera est

'Medicine for the dead is too late' – Quintillian. See *Quintillian*.

Medicine

The science and art of healing – from *mederi*, 'to attend to someone'. Medicine is the name given to the science of diagnosing, treating or preventing disease and illness of the body and mind. Generally, it utilizes drugs, diet, exercise and other non-surgical means to do so. Hippocrates is considered to be the father of orthodox western medicine.

Medicus curat, natura sanat

'The doctor cares (for his patient), nature heals (him).'

Melaena
Black stools – from the New Latin *melena*, itself from the Greek *melas*, 'black'. This is the name given to the passage of black, tarry stools composed largely of blood that has been acted on by gastric juices after a haemorrhage somewhere along the digestive tract.

Melancholia
The old name for depression – from the Greek *melas*, 'black', and *chole*, 'bile'. This curious name is very ancient and was described by the Ancient Greek physicians. It refers to the Doctrine of Humors and the belief that lowness of spirits was due to an excess of the humour (fluid) known as black bile. See *The Anatomy of Melancholia, doctrine of humors* and *involutional melancholia*.

Melanin
Dark (black) skin pigment, which in clumps forms moles or freckles – from the Greek *melas*, 'black'.

Membrum virile
'Male member.' A Latin euphemism for the penis.

Memento mori
'Remember that you are mortal.' Essentially, everything is transient – fame, health, life itself. In ancient Rome, the phrase is said to have been used on the occasions when a Roman general was parading through the streets of Rome. A servant would stand behind the general and remind him with the phrase *memento mori* that today he may be a god, but tomorrow was another day and he might be dead!

Memoria technical

'An artificial memory.' This implies the use of some artificial means of remembering vast amounts of
information. Mnemonics are an example, as used by
many medical students when trying to master the names
of the muscles, arteries and nerves of the body.

Menopause

The end of the female reproductive age – from the Greek
menos, 'a month' and the Latin *pausa*, 'stopping'.

Menses

The female periods – from the Greek *menos*, 'a month'.
See *menstruation*.

Mensque pati durum sustinet aegra nihil

'A sick mind cannot endure any hard treatment' – Ovid.
See *Ovid*.

Mens sana in corpore sano

'A healthy mind in a healthy body.' This famous quotation is slightly out of context. As quoted here, it appears
to say that a healthy body is the prerequisite for a healthy
mind or spirit, but that's not how it was meant initially.
The complete quote is *orandum est ut sit mens sana in
corpore sano*, which means 'let's hope that there is a
healthy spirit in a healthy body', or 'a sound mind in a
sound body is a thing to be prayed for' – Juvenal, *Satires*
10, 356. See *Juvenal*.

Menstruation

'The monthly flow', from the Latin *menstruationis*. See
menses.

Metabolism
The internal chemistry and energetics of the body – from the Greek *meta*, 'after' and the Greek *bole*, 'throwing'.

Metacarpal
The long bones of the hand – from *meta*, 'after', and *carpus*, 'wrist'.

Metatarsals
The long foot bones – from the Greek *meta*, 'after', and the Greek *tarsus*, 'ankle'.

Micturition
To pass urine, from the Latin *micturire* 'to urinate'.

Micturition syncope
A faint resulting from straining to pass urine – from *micturire*, 'to urinate' and *syncope*. This is actually a very common cause of fainting, since a stretched bladder literally gives the feeling that one is 'bursting for a wee'. The sudden release of pressure causes the faint. See *syncope*.

Misce fiat mistura
'Mix and let a mixture be made.' In prescription-writing the abbreviation *m. ft. mist.* would be used when the doctor wished the chemist to make up a mixture with certain ingredients.

Mistura
'Mixture' to be given. In prescription-writing the abbreviation *Mist.* could be used when a mixture is to be dispensed.

Mitis

'Weak.' In prescription-writing the abbreviation *mit.* would be used if a weak solution or mixture was to be made and dispensed.

Mitral valve

A bicuspid valve inside the heart, through which oxygenated blood passes from the left atrium to the left ventricle – from *mitralis*, 'two-pointed', *mitra*, 'bishop's hat', and *valva*, 'door'. The mitral valve is the only two-cusped valve of the four heart valves. If the valve is incompetent – mitral incompetence – then blood can flow backwards. If the valve is too narrow – mitral stenosis – then it may be associated with irregularity of the heart beat. Both can ultimately lead to heart failure.

Mitte

'Send.' In prescription-writing this indicates the amount that should be sent to the patient. For example, *Mitte 20 caps*, means dispense 20 capsules of whatever drug is being prescribed. See *prescription*.

Modus omnibus in rebus optimum est habitu

'Moderation in all things is the best of rules' – Plautus. See *Habet natura, ut aliarum omnium rerum, sic vivendi modum, Plautus.*

Modus operandi

'The way of operating.' This has come to be associated with the method by which a crime has been committed. It also is of relevance to the work of the surgeon.

Mollis

'Soft.' In prescription-writing the abbreviation *moll.* would be used if, for example soft tablets were to be dispensed.

Molluscum contagiosum

A viral infection of the skin (by the organism called *Molluscum contagiosum* virus MSV), producing character-istic lesions that, on close inspection, look like snail shells. It is spread by contact and is quite contagious in children, hence its name. From *molluscum*, 'thin-shelled' (and snail-like) and *contingere*, 'to have contact with, pollute'.

Mons pubis or mons veneris

'The female mound of Venus', the rounded area above the pubic bone. It is in fact a pad of fatty tissue, which is richly supplied with sensory nerves. Both names are used in anatomy, *mons pubis* giving a true anatomical description, *mons veneris* quaintly indicating its associa-tion with the goddess of love.

More dicto

'In the manner directed.' In prescription-writing the abbreviation *m.d.* would be used to mean in the manner directed. This sort of prescription is not favoured nowa-days because it is open to misinterpretation. The same applies to *more dicto applicandum*, *more solito* and *more dicto utendum*.

More dicto utendum (m.d.u.), 'to be used as directed'.

More dicto applicandum (m.d.applic.), 'to be applied as directed'.

More solito (m.sol.), 'in the usual manner'.

Morphine

A narcotic drug, an alkaloid of opium. The name comes from Morpheus, the Greek god of dreams.

Mucus

Phlegm or mucus – from the Latin word for 'slime'. Mucus is the name given to the slimy coating on epithelial or mucus membranes in the body. It is secreted by various 'goblet cells' in the digestive and respiratory tracts in order to lubricate the membranes. It is rich in mucins and inorganic salts, and is essential to the healthy functioning of the body. In many ailments, from the common cold to acute bronchitis, excess mucus is produced. In these cases the individual usually finds the symptom of excess mucus or phlegm an unpleasant nuisance, but it is in fact one of the body's ways of protecting itself.

Multum in parvo

'Much in little.' In the context of a placebo, it may be that the smaller the pill, the greater the perceived effect. A less-is-more principle. Homoeopathy could be the ultimate *multum in parvo* effect.

Muscle

Little mouse – from the Latin word for 'small mouse', *musculus*. The Romans thought that rippling muscles looked like little mice moving under the skin. There are in fact about 650 muscles in the human body and their general function is to move things around the body or to move the body itself. There are three types of muscle. The first is smooth muscle which occurs in layers around or along internal organs. An example is the smooth muscle of the intestine, responsible for moving food and digestive products along the digestive tract. Smooth muscle operates involuntarily or automatically under instructions from the nervous system. Cardiac muscle is the very specialized muscle of the heart, which pumps non-stop throughout your life. Skeletal muscles are the muscles that enable us to move our bodies and which look good when you flex your biceps. They are the 'mice under the skin' that the Romans so admired. They are entirely under conscious control.

Musica est mentis medicina moestae
'Music is medicine for a sick mind.'

Myalgia encephalomyelitis
Chronic fatigue syndrome – literally painful muscles and inflammation of the brain and spinal cord. From the Greek words *myos*, 'muscles', *algos*, 'pain', *egkephalos*, 'the brain' and *myelos*, 'spinal cord'. This is a pseudo-pathological description of the state of profound fatigue that seems to come on after a viral infection, vaccine or trauma of some kind. It is little understood by the medical profession.

Myocardial infarction
Heart attack – from myocardial, 'to do with the myocardium', and the Latin *infarctionis*, 'stuffed until full'.

Myocardium
The muscle of the heart – from the Greek *myo*, 'muscle', and *kardia*, 'heart'.

N

Narcolepsy
A sleeping seizure – from the Greek *narke*, 'stupor', and *lepsis*, 'a seizure'. A sleep disorder in which the individual falls asleep at inappropriate times. It could be very dangerous if the individual is driving or operating machinery.

Narcotic
A drug that induces stupor – a powerful painkiller, like heroin or morphine.

Nasal
To do with the nose – from *nasalis*, 'of the nose'. We use this term to describe all things to do with the nose, whether that is to describe the nasal septum, the cartilage that separates the two sides of the nose; nasal polyps, which obstruct the nose; or nasal speech.

Nascentes morimur
'Every day we die a little' – Manilius. See *Manilius*.

Natal
To do with birth – from *natalis*, 'appertaining to birth'.

Nausea
Sickness – coined by Hippocrates, meaning 'like seasickness', from the Greek word *naus*, meaning 'ship'.

Nauseum gravidarum

Nausea in pregnancy. This is the natural sickness that most expectant mothers experience, as opposed to the more dangerous *hyperemesis gravidarum*, which is excessive nausea and vomiting, often necessitating hospitalization and medical treatment.

Nebula

'A spray'. In prescription-writing the abbreviation *neb.* could be used to indicate that a spray is to be dispensed. Nowadays there may be some confusion because both sprays and nebulas are prescribed. Nebules are special capsules for use in a nebulizer. This is a special gadget for producing a fine spray for inhalation when treating someone, usually an asthmatic, during an acute breathing problem.

Necrophilia

Love of the dead – from the Greek *nekros,* 'dead' and *philia,* 'love'. One of the paraphilias. See *paraphilia.*

Necrosis

Death of tissue – from the Greek *nekros,* 'dead', and *osis,* 'condition'.

Neque ignorare medicum oportet quae sit aegri natura

'Nor does it behove the doctor to ignore the sick man's temperament' – Cornelius Celsus, *De Medicina.* Here, Celsus is telling the doctor to take account of the constitution and the temperament of the patient. By this he is referring to the Doctrine of Humors theory of his time. See *Celsus, Doctrine of Humors.*

Ne quid nimis

'Nothing in excess' – Terence. The Romans were well aware of the dangers of excess and this maxim appears in many forms, having been written about by Cicero and Plautus, to name two. See *Terence*.

Nervi erigentes

The excitory nerves that stimulate clitoris and penis to become erect.

Nil desperandum

'Never despair' – Horace, *Odes*. Essentially, Horace means that one should never give up, things are never as bad as you think. See *Horace*.

Nil similius insano quam ebrius

'There is nothing more like a madman than a drunken person.'

Nocebo

A negative placebo – literally, 'I will harm'. A nocebo effect is an ill effect caused by the suggestion or belief that something is harmful. Some people will anticipate a side effect and will develop one. Superstitions and curses could operate because of the nocebo effect. See *placebo*.

Nocte

Take 'at night'. In prescription-writing the word *nocte*, or the abbreviation *noct.* or *nocte.* may be used to mean take the remedy last thing at night.

Nocte et mane

'Night and morning.' In prescription-writing the abbreviation *n. et m.* is used when a drug is to be taken night and morning. **Nocte maneque** *(n. mque)* could also be used and means the same.

Non compos mentis
'Not of sound mind.'

Non est in medico semper relevetur ut aeger
'It is not always in the physician's power to cure the sick person' – Ovid. See *Ovid* .

Non repetatur
'Do not repeat.' In prescription-writing the abbreviation *non.rep.* could be used to indicate that the prescription is to be issued once only, and not be used as a repeat prescription without first seeing the doctor.

Non sinet esse feros
'It is forbidden to be cruel.' Motto of the Royal College of Physicians of Edinburgh. This is a strange motto to adopt, but there has been debate over the years as to how the motto was chosen. Much depends upon how one translates *feros* ('cruel', 'savage'). It appears to be an extract from a poem by Ovid, but with the alteration of the original word *nec* ('and not', or 'but not') to *non* ('not'). The essence of the motto, however, is that application of study will yield the best results for the patient.

Nota bene
'Take notice.' This is often used to emphasize a point in medical texts and papers by the abbreviation N.B.

Nulla res tam necessaria est quam medicina
'Nothing is so necessary as medicine.'

O

Obit
'He, or she, died'.

Oblique muscles of the eye
There are two oblique muscles attached to each eyeball: the inferior oblique and superior oblique muscles. Whereas the rectus muscles of the eye control up, down and sidewards movements, the oblique muscles control the rotation of the eye during angled viewing.

Obsta principiis
Nip it in the bud. A surgical principle. It is better to deal with a pathological condition before it has had time to grow and spread.

Occiput
The bone at the back of the skull – from *oc*, 'behind', and *caput*, 'head'.

Occult
Hidden – from *oc*, 'behind', and *cultus*, 'hidden'. This has nothing whatever to do with magic and things mysterious. In medicine it means that something is hidden or not visible to the naked eye. Occult blood in the bowel motions is not visible but its presence is highly significant. Similarly, occult blood may be present in the urine

but will only be detected by special dip-testing sticks or by microscopic examination.

Oculi, tanquam speculatores, altissimum locum obtinent

'The eyes, like sentinels, hold the highest place in the body' – Cicero. See *Cicero* .

Oculus dexter

'Right eye.' In prescription-writing the abbreviation *o.d.* could be used when eye drops are to be applied to the right eye. However, it is considered preferable to write out the words 'right eye' nowadays, since the abbreviation *o.d.* is often used to indicate that something should be used once daily.

Oculus sinister

'Left eye.' In prescription-writing the abbreviation *o.s.* could be used when eye drops are to be applied to the left eye.

Oculo ultra

'Both eyes.' In prescription-writing the abbreviation *o.u.* could be used when eye drops are to be applied to both eyes.

Odontoid process

The pivot that is shaped like a tooth – from *odontos*, 'tooth' and the Greek, *–oid*, 'shaped like', and the Latin *pro*, 'in front of' and *cessus*, 'a going' (a process is essentially a projecting piece or peg that acts as a pivot). The odontoid process, or pegs, has nothing to do with the teeth. It is a piece of bone that sticks out from the second cervical vertebra. It allows the first cervical vertebra, the Atlas, to rotate, so that the skull can turn. See *Atlas*.

Oedipus

In Classical Mythology Oedipus was the son of King Laius of Thebes and Queen Jocasta. When he was born it was prophesised that he would kill his father. Terrified by the prophesy King Laius had his infant son taken away with the intention that he be left to die in the wilderness. The king's servant could not bring himself to do this, however, and gave the child to a shepherd, who in turn presented Oedipus to King Polybus of Corinth and Queen Merope. They brought him up as their own son. Later, Oedipus was told of the prophesy by the Delphic Oracle, so he left Corinth believing that if he were to stay he could kill Polybus, whom he thought to be his real father. While on his travels he met and killed Laius in an argument, without being aware that the man he killed was his father and the King of Thebes. After that he saved Thebes by answering the riddle of the Sphinx. His reward was to become King of Thebes and to take the hand in marriage of the recently widowed queen, Jocasta. Although the couple had four children, they did not live happily. Misfortune after misfortune occurred and Thebes became a polluted and disease-ridden city. A soothsayer finally revealed that Oedipus was the cause of the ill fortune, because he had killed his father and married his mother. Jocasta committed suicide and Oedipus blinded himself. Sigmund Freud took the tale of Oedipus and adapted it as an explanation for the development of the Superego, Id and Ego. The Oedipus Complex, he postulated, was the childhood desire to sleep with the mother and kill the father. See *Sphincter*.

Olecranon

The point of the elbow – from the Greek *olene*, 'elbow', and *kranion*, 'head'. The olecranon is the pointed end of the ulna, which fits into the olecranon fossa of the humerus. See *humerus*.

Olecranon bursitis

Swelling of the elbow – from the Greek *olene*, 'elbow', *kranion*, 'head', and the Greek *bursa*, 'a sac'. This painful swelling is the equivalent of housemaid's knee but in the elbow. Cynics suggest it is common in drinkers who spend too much time leaning at the bar.

Olfactory

The sense of smell – from *olefacere*, 'to cause to smell'.

Olfactory nerve

The nerve of the sense of smell – from *olefacere*, 'to cause to smell'. The olfactory nerve is the first of the twelve cranial nerves.

Oligospermia

Few sperm – from the Greek *oligos*, 'few' and the Greek *sperma*, 'seeds'. A low sperm count on seminal analysis may be a cause of subfertility.

Omentum

Fat bowels – from the Latin *omentum*, 'fatty bowel'. The omentum is a name given to the tissues inside the abdomen, which hold, tether and yet protect the intestines. They often contain great quantities of adipose or fat tissue.

Omne nocte
'Every night.' In prescription-writing the abbreviation *o.m.* would be used to indicate that a drug is to be taken every night.

Omne quadrante hora
'Every quarter of an hour.' In prescription-writing the abbreviation *om.quad. hor.* could be used to indicate that something was to be given or taken every quarter of an hour. This is a very frequent dosage interval but the term is unlikely to be used or understood nowadays. It is just as easy to write it in English in words and figures.

Omnes ab omnibus discamus
'Let us learn all things from everybody.' Motto of the Association of Surgeons of Great Britain and Ireland. Perhaps it should be from 'every body', rather than from everybody.

Omnes homines sibi sanitatem cupiunt, saepe autem omnia, quae valetudini contraria sunt, faciunt
'All men wish to be healthy, but often they do everything that's disadvantageous to their health.' How true!

Omne tertia hora
'Every three hours.' In prescription-writing the abbreviation *om. tert. hor* could be used to indicate that a remedy was to be taken every three hours. This term is unlikely to be used or understood nowadays. It is just as easy to write it in English in words and figures.

Omnium artium medicina nobilissima est
'Medicine is the noblest of all arts.'

Oncology
The study of tumours – from the Greek *onkos*, 'tumour', and the Greek *logos*, 'the study of something'.

Onychogryphosis
Overgrown fingernails or toenails – from the Greek *onychos*, 'fingernails' or 'toenails', and the Greek *gryphos*, 'curved or hooked', and the Greek *osis*, 'condition'.

Ophthalma neonatorum
Inflammation of the eye in the newborn – from *ophalmos*, 'eye' and *neonatorum*, 'newborn'. This condition comes about when a baby contracts an infection from the mother's tissues as it passes through the birth canal.

Ophthalmology
The study of the eye and diseases of the eye – from the Greek *ophthalmos*, 'eye', and the Greek *logos*, 'the study of something'.

Opifer que per orbem dicor
'I am spoken of all over the world as one who brings help.' Motto of the Worshipful Society of Apothecaries of London, taken from the first book of Ovid's *Metamorphoses*. See *Ovid*.

Opprobrium medicorum
'The reproach of physicians.' This referred to incurable diseases, specifically gout, which in days gone by defied treatment.

Optic
Of the eye – from the Greek *optikos*, 'to do with sight'. We use this term to describe things that are to do with the eye and sight. In anatomy we talk about the optic nerve

which is the nerve that supplies the eye and which transmits visual images to the brain, along the optic pathway. Interestingly, the visual cortex, the part of the brain that perceives vision, is based at the back of the brain, not at the front as most people imagine.

Optic nerve
The nerve of sight – from the Greek *optikos*, 'to do with sight'. The optic nerve is the second of the twelve cranial nerves.

Optimum medicamentum quies est
'Peace is the best medicine.'

Orbicularis oculi
The eye closing muscle – from *orbicularis*, 'circular or disc-shaped' and *oculus*, 'eye'. A ring muscle with a sphincter-like action surrounds each eye, and screws it closed to produce the little 'crow's foot' wrinkles to the sides of the eye.

Orbicularis oris
The mouth-closing or pouting muscle – from *orbicularis*, 'circular or disc-shaped', and *oris*, 'mouth'. The ring muscle with a sphincter-like action that lies within the lips and surrounds the mouth, to close it in a pouting fashion. There are five muscles around it, which pull the mouth into different facial expressions.

Orchitis
Inflammation of the testicle – from the Greek *orchis*, 'testicle', and *itis*, 'inflammation of something'. Orchitis can occur during mumps and result in subfertility when contracted in adulthood. Hence the desirability of contracting mumps in childhood, and the reason for

immunizing young men against the condition. This is a good example of the use of the Greek for a pathological condition and the Latin for the anatomical structure. See *testis and testicle*.

Organ
Organ – from *organum*, 'engine'. An organ is a functional unit of the body, such as the heart, liver, kidney.

Orifice
Mouth-like – from *orificium*, 'mouth-like'. An orifice is the opening into the body, or the opening in an organ or gland. The main external orifices are: the nostrils, used in breathing and the sense of smell; the mouth, for eating and for speech; the ear canals for hearing; the anus for defecation, the urethra for urination; and the vagina in females for sexual intercourse and for childbirth. Internal orifices are openings into organs or glands, such as the vermiform appendix orifice, which connects the caecum with the appendix.

Orthopaedics
The speciality that looks after bones and fractures – from *orthos*, 'straight', and the Greek *paidikos*, meaning 'to do with children'. Originally, orthopaedics was to do with straightening deformities in children and general bone setting. It now deals with all of the musculoskeletal system (at all ages) and has made incredible advances in the replacement of joints.

Os
This term has two meanings in anatomy:

1. Mouth of (something) – from *oris*, 'mouth'. The *os uterus* is the mouth or opening of the *uterus*, 'womb'.

2. Bone – from *ossis*, 'bone'. The *os sacrum* consists of the five fused sacral, vertebrae, the *os calcis* is the heel bone and the *os Vesalianum*, an extra small foot bone. This last is of particular interest because it is not present in everyone, but was described by the great anatomist Andreas Vesalius in his ground-breaking anatomical textbook and atlas *De Humani Corporis Fabrica Librorum Septem*, published in 1543. See *Vesalius*.

Os capitatum

The capitate bone, the third bone in the distal row of wrist bones – from the Latin *caput*, meaning 'head'. It has a rounded head that fits into the hollowed-out part of the scaphoid bone.

Os hamatum

The hamate bone, the fourth bone in the distal row of wrist bones – from the Latin *hamatum*, 'hooked'.

Os lunatum

The lunate bone, the second bone in the proximal row of wrist bones – from the Latin *lunatis*, 'moon-shaped'.

Os pisiformis

The pisiform bone, the fourth bone in the proximal row of wrist bones – from the Latin *pisum*, 'pea', and *formis*, meaning 'shaped like'. It is a pea-shaped and pea-sized little bone.

Os scaphoideum

The scaphoid bone, the first wrist bone of the proximal row (see *carpus*) on the thumb side – from the Greek *skaphe*, meaning 'a hollowed out boat, a skiff'. This little bone is often injured when one falls on the outstretched hand in an attempt to break the fall. It is located in what the old anatomists called the 'anatomical snuff box', the little depression on the wrist when the thumb is adducted, or drawn up as far as possible in the same plane as the hand.

Os trapezium
The trapezium bone, the first bone in the distal row of wrist bones, situated between the scaphoid bone and the first metacarpal, thumb bone. The name comes from the Greek *trapeza*, meaning 'table'.

Os trapezoid
The trapezoid bone, the second bone in the distal row of wrist bones – from the Greek *trapezion*, 'little table', and *oid*, 'like'. It is a smaller version of its neighbour the os trapezium.

Os triquetrum
The triquetrum bone, the third bone in the proximal row of wrist bones – from the Latin *triquetrus*, 'three-cornered'. It actually looks like a small pyramid.

Ossicles
Little bones – from *ossiculinum*, 'little bone'. There are three tiny bones in the middle ear. These are the *malleus* 'hammer', *incus* 'anvil' and *stapes* 'stirrup'. Each is shaped like the word that describes it. In hearing, the eardrum vibrates and causes the malleus (hammer) to 'fall on' or vibrate the incus (anvil) to move the stapes (stirrup) and thus transmit sound across the middle ear to the inner ear.

Otitis externa

'Inflammation of the outer ear' – from the Greek *otos*, 'ear'. This is the name for inflammation, a type of dermatitis of the outer ear and the ear canal.

Otitis media

'Inflammation of the middle ear.' This is a painful inflammation of the middle ear chamber, often with the accumulation of fluid or pus inside the chamber.

Otorhinolaryngology

The study of the ear, nose and throat – from the Greek *otos*, 'ear', and the Greek *rhinos*, 'nose', and the Greek *laryngos*, 'throat' and the Greek *logos*, 'the study of something'. The old name for ear, nose and throat (ENT) surgery.

Ovid

Publius Ovidius Naso (43 BCE–AD 17) was a Roman poet who wrote on topics of love, abandoned women, and mythology. His greatest work, the *Metamorphoses*, enjoyed huge popularity. He was banished to Tomis in the Black Sea by the Emperor Augustus, reportedly because Augustus was offended by his work *Ars Amatoria*, although it is more likely that it was because of an affair he had with a relative of the emperor. He died in exile.

Ovi vitellus

'The yolk of an egg.' Surprisingly, this could be included in prescriptions in days gone by, because egg yolks containing nutrients were considered a good base for a tonic.

Ovum

'Egg' – from the Latin word *ovum* – plural *ova*.

P

Panacea
'A cure-all' – from the Greek goddess Panacea, reputedly one of Asclepius's two daughters. She was considered to be the goddess of healing. In days gone by people sought a cure-all, or a panacea that would cure all ills. The famous Theriac, or Venice, treacle contained sixty-four ingredients and was much favoured in the fifteenth and sixteenth centuries. The medicine shows of the American West were vehicles for 'snake-oil' operators who peddled panaceas that they claimed would cure everything from baldness to apoplexy. Aesculapius would have turned in his grave, if gods had graves.

Pancreas
The organ that produces insulin and the enzyme amylase – from the Greek words *pan*, 'all', and *kreas*, 'meat'. The pancreas of hunted animals was considered by early Greeks as a delicacy, a sweetbread. It is situated in the bend of the duodenum. It produces amylase, the enzyme that breaks fats down and the hormone insulin, which regulates the blood sugar.

Paralysis
A weakening of a part to the point of loss of function, temporary or otherwise – from the Greek words *para*, 'beside' and *lysis*, 'weakening'. Paralysis means a loss

of muscle function, of one or more muscle groups. It can be a localized paralysis of a specific type, such as Bell's Palsy, which causes loss of muscle function on one side of the face, due to inflammation of the facial nerve, the seventh cranial nerve. It can be paralysis of one side of the body, a hemiplegia after a stroke. It can be paralysis of the lower part of the body, a paraplegia after damage to the lower spinal cord.

Paraphilia

Literally, 'love beyond the normal', from the Latin *para*, 'beyond', and the Greek *philia*, 'love'. A paraphilia is the name given to a condition in which the individual's sexual arousal and gratification is dependent upon fantasizing about and engaging in behaviour that is atypical and often extreme. It may involve fetishes, or be focused upon particular age groups, such as children (paedophilia), the elderly (gerontophilia), or even the deceased (necrophilia). Obviously, some paraphilias may bring people into conflict with society, so there may be ethical and potential medico-legal issues relating to them.

Paraplegia

Paralysis of the lower part of the body, commonly affecting both legs and often internal organs below the waist. From the Greek words *para*, meaning 'beside', and *plege*, meaning 'a blow' or a 'stroke'.

Parotid

The large salivary gland in the cheek – from the Greek words *para*, 'beside', and *otos*, 'ear'. This gland becomes infected in mumps, hence its correct name of *infectious parotitis*.

Pars sanitas velle sanari fuit

'It was a sign of health that he was willing to be cured' – Seneca, *Hippolytus*, Act 1, 249. See *Seneca*.

Partes aequales

'Equal parts.' In prescription-writing the abbreviation *part. aeq.* could be used to indicate that something was to be made available in equal parts. Nowadays many medications are prepacked, because bioavailability (standardized amounts of drugs) is of paramount importance. This term is unlikely to be used nowadays.

Parti dolente

'To the painful part.' In prescription-writing the abbreviation *part.dol.* could be used to indicate that an ointment, cream or embrocation was to be applied to the painful part of the body.

Patella

The kneecap – from *patella*, meaning 'saucer'. It sits like a reversed saucer on the front of the knee joint.

Pathogen

A disease producing agent – from the Greek words, *pathos*, 'disease', and *gen*, 'making'. A bacterium, fungus or virus can be a pathogen. Cigarette smoking is said to be pathogenic, or a disease producing habit.

Pathology

The study of disease and its effects on the body – from the Greek words *pathos*, 'disease', and *logos*, 'study of'. Pathology used to be called morbid anatomy, meaning the study of the anatomical tissues after death.

Pectoralis muscles
The chest muscles which rotate the arm inwards – from the Latin *pectus*, meaning 'chest'. There are two pectoral muscles on each side, *pectoralis major* and *pectoralis minor*, one on top of the other, the so-called 'pecs' so beloved of body-builders.

Pectus
'The chest.' In prescription-writing the abbreviation *pect.* could be used to indicate that something was to be applied to the chest. This relates to the days before modern pharmacology when external applications like poultices, blisters and plasters were used for internal conditions.

Pelvis
The pelvis is the bony bowl that contains the reproductive organs and the lower intestines, etc. It comes from the Latin *pelvis*, meaning 'wide bowl'.

Penis
The male organ – from the Latin *penis*, meaning 'a tail', itself derived from *pendere*, 'to hang down'. The penis is the external male organ which has the dual function of urination and sexual intercourse. In order to have sexual intercourse the penis has to become erect, which it does when the Corpus spongiosum and Corpus cavernosum become engorged with blood. Interestingly, the accepted anatomical position of the penis is not hanging down, but standing erect. This can be checked by looking at the long vein which runs down the back of the penis, which is called the dorsal vein of the penis. When the penis is erect, this vein will be found facing the abdominal wall, that is, it will be

pointing towards the back as the tip of the penis points upwards. See *Corpus cavernosum* and *Corpus spongiosum*.

Per diem
'Take daily.' In prescription writing *per diem* means to take a medicine at the same time each day.

Per os
'By mouth.' In prescription-writing the abbreviation *p.o.* could be used when something is to be taken by mouth.

Per rectum
'By rectum.' In prescription-writing the abbreviation *p.r.* could be used when a drug is to be delivered via the back passage. This is the favoured route for certain drugs if they are considered to irritate the stomach. It is actually a very good passage for the absorption of drugs.

Per scientiam ad salutem aegroti
'To heal the sick through knowledge.'

Per se
'By itself, intrinsically.' This is often used in texts and papers.

Per testes
'By witnesses.' See *testis and testicle*.

Per vagina
'By vagina.' In prescription-writing the abbreviation *p.v.* could be used when a drug is to be given via the vagina. This could be a cream or a pessary.

Pes

'The foot' – from the Latin word *pes*. *Pes cavus*, claw foot, and *pes planus*, flat foot.

Pessus

'A pessary.' In prescription-writing the abbreviation *pess.* could be used to indicate that a pessary, a pellet for insertion in the vagina is to be used.

Phalynx or (plural) phalanges

The small finger and toe bones – from the Greek *phalanx*, and plural *phalanges*, meaning 'soldiers in close order'.

Pharmaca das aegroto; aurum tibi porrigit aeger. Tu morbum curas illius, ille tuum

'You give medicine to a sick man; the sick man hands you gold in return. You cure his disease, he cures yours.'

Pharmacopoeia

An official publication dealing with the recognized drugs, giving their doses, preparations, sources, side-effects, etc. – from the Greek *pharmakopoiia*, meaning 'creation or preparation of drugs'. Thus you have the American Pharmacopoeia, the European Pharmacopoeia and the British Pharmacopoeia.

Pharyngotympanic tube

The Eustachian tube – from the Greek *pharyngos*, 'throat', and the Greek *tympanum*, meaning 'drum'. This tube connects the middle-ear chamber with the back of the throat. Its function is to equalize pressure between the middle ear chamber and the outer atmosphere. It is this action that causes one's ears to pop when altering altitude. It was discovered and described by the Italian

anatomist Bartolomeo Eustachi in the sixteenth century.
See *Eustachi, Bartolomeo*.

Phiala prius agitate

'The bottle having been shaken.' In prescription-writing
the abbreviation *p.p.a.* could be used to indicate that a
bottle containing a mixture should be shaken before a dose
is taken, to ensure that the mixture is uniform throughout.

Physician

From the Greek *physikos*, meaning 'regarding nature'. It
relates to the early Greek philosophers who studied
nature and taught medicine. In some countries, notably
the USA, the word 'physician' is used interchangeably
with the word 'doctor'. In this context it comes about
because the person practised the art or science of physic,
the old term for medicine. In the UK on the other hand
the word doctor is used when referring to a medical
practitioner, while the word physician is used in reference to a specialist in the field of internal medicine.

Physiology

The study of physical function – from the Greek words
physis, 'natural life' and *logos*, 'study of'.

Pietate, arte et scientia corrigere

'With compassion, skill and knowledge we correct,
straighten or set straight.' Motto of the Canadian
Orthopaedic Association. And a very appropriate motto
it is, too.

Pilula

'A pill.' In prescription-writing the abbreviation *pil.* is
used to indicate that pills are to be dispensed.

Pineal

A cone-shaped organ within the brain – from *pinea*, 'pine cone'. The pineal gland in the brain produces serotonin and melatonin, two hormones. Its function is still somewhat mysterious. People with a poor sense of direction often have calcified pineal glands, whereas those with a good sense of direction and spacial sense seem to have a non-calcified large pineal gland. Homing pigeons seem to have huge pineal glands.

Pituitary gland

A cyst-like structure at the base of the brain that governs all of the major endocrine (hormone) glands in the body. From the Latin *pituita*, meaning 'mucous maker'. The Roman physician Galen (AD 129–199) taught that mucus from the nose came from the brain, from the mucus-like cyst that we now recognize as the pituitary gland. Modern physiology now knows that nasal mucus is produced by the nose, whereas the pituitary gland operates the thyroid, adrenals, ovaries and testicles.

Placebo

An ineffective drug or treatment that somehow makes the patient feel better – from *placere*, 'to please'. The placebo effect is a fascinating phenomenon, possibly the most fascinating phenomenon in medicine. For some reason (possibly for many reasons) an individual will respond to an inactive agent in a very positive manner. Nowadays placebos are used in scientific trials, usually double-blind trials, in which neither the patient nor the doctor knows whether they are being given an active agent or a placebo. This sort of trial is used to assess whether a drug (the active agent) is superior to the placebo, i.e. better than nothing. The problem is that a placebo response can occur in anything between twenty-five and seventy per cent of cases. The frequently reported placebo response is thirty per cent but it depends upon many factors. In general, the more dramatic the treatment, the greater the placebo response. Surgery, being the most dramatic type of treatment, should therefore have the highest placebo response. Perhaps it does, but most surgeons do not like being told this. In studies on medicines it has been found that red, yellow or brown tablets or capsules work best, whereas green and blue work less well. It has also been found that the smaller the tablets or pills the better, on the principle of *multum in parvo*. In days gone by placebos were prescribed liberally. The Latin names may have helped boost their efficacy. For example, *tinctura cardamomi compositae* (a mixture of cayenne pepper, caraway, cochineal, glycerin and alcohol), or *tinctura cinchonae compositae* (a mixture of quinine, orange peel, cochineal and alcohol) both worked well as tonics and were extremely popular. Nowadays placebos can still be prescribed on the NHS, in the form of acid (or alkaline) gentian mixture. See *multum in parvo* and *nocebo*.

Plasmodium

The protozoal parasites that cause malaria – from *plasma*, 'moulded thing' and the Greek *odes*, 'resembling'. The parasites infect the red blood cells and produce a characteristic paroxysm (chill and fever) at periodic intervals. *Plasmodium falciparum* causes malignant tertian malaria, the most serious type. *Plasmodium vivax* and the much rarer *plasmodium ovale* cause benign tertian malaria, and *plasmodium malariae* causes benign quartan malaria. See *fever* and *malaria*.

Platysma

A broad, thin muscle on each side of the neck, extending from the upper part of the shoulder to the corner of the mouth, the action of which wrinkles the skin of the neck and depresses the corner of the mouth. It is in fact a vestigial remnant of the *panniculus carnosus* of animals (which allows the horse to flick a fly off its back) and comes from the Greek word meaning 'plate'.

Plautus

Titus Maccius Plautus (circa 254 BCE–184 BCE) was a comic playwright who has left us some twenty-four plays. His most typical character is the clever slave who manipulates his master, forming the model for many later writers, including Shakespeare. The popular TV show *Up Pompeii* was based on his work.

Plexus

A braid, a tangle, from *plexus*, meaning 'braid'. A tangle or network of nerves or blood vessels. There are numerous nerve plexuses in the body, responsible for innervating limbs or important structures.

- The *brachial plexus* (from *brachialis*, meaning 'of the arm') the main network of nerves supplying the upper limb. Nerve roots pass from the neck and upper thorax, join together and pass through in the axilla (armpit) then divide to supply nerves to the various parts of the arm and hand.
- The *sacral plexus* is the equivalent network for the lower limb, the main nerve formed being the sciatic nerve.
- *The solar plexus* is the lay name given to the coeliac plexus.

Pliny the Elder

Gaius Plinius (AD23–79) was a prodigious writer, cavalry officer and provincial governor. He had in his time been counsellor to emperors Vespasian and Titus. He wrote volumes on natural history, war, weapons, contemporary history and rhetoric. His great work was *Naturalis Historia*. He died of suffocation while making first-hand observations of the eruption of Mount Vesuvius, which destroyed the city of Pompei in AD 79. He was quite categoric in his dismissal of the possibility of an afterlife.

Pliny the Younger

Gaius Plinius Caecilius Secundas (AD 66–112) was the nephew and adopted son of Pliny the Elder. He was a lawyer, writer and orator. He served the Emperor Trajan as a provincial governor. His famous letters (*epistulae*) to Trajan and Tacitus filled ten volumes.

Plus a medico quam a morbo periculi

'More of danger from the physician than from the disease.' In the early years of the Roman Empire physicians and their abilities were held in low esteem.

Poculum

'A cup.' In prescription-writing the abbreviation *poc.* could be used to indicate that a remedy is to be taken in a cup of liquid, usually water.

Pone aurum

'Behind the ear.' In prescription-writing the abbreviation *pon. aur.* could be used to indicate that an ointment or cream was to be applied behind the ear.

Post cibos
'After food.' In prescription-writing the abbreviation *p.c* is used to indicate that a medicine must be taken after food. This is usually because the medication has a known gastritis-like side effect, which may be countered by the presence of food in the stomach.

Post epulas stabis vel passus mille meabis
'After meals you should either stand or walk a mile' – maxim of Salerno School of Health. See *Salerno School of Health*.

Post prandium
'After eating a meal (dinner).' This is a common time to test blood glucose levels to see how the body is handling its sugar.

Post prandium stabis, post coenum ambulabis
'Rest after lunch; after supper walk' – maxim of Salerno School of Health. See *Salerno School of Health*.

Post meridiem
'After noon.'

Post mortem
'After death.'

Post partum
'After birth.'

Potest exercitatio et temperantia etiam in senecutute conservare aliquid pristini roboris
'Exercise and temperance can preserve something of our early strength even in old age' – Cicero. See *Cicero*.

Praesente medico nihil nocet

'In the presence of a doctor nothing can harm.'

Praestat cautela quam medela

'Precaution is better than cure.' Another Latin maxim whose wisdom cannot be disputed.

Prescription

The doctor's instructions – from *prae*, 'before', and *scribere*, 'to write'. A prescription traditionally has four components:

- The superscription or heading, which starts with the abbreviation *Rx*, from the Latin *recipe*, meaning 'take (thou)'.
- The inscription, which contains the names of the medicines or drugs and their quantities. Often abbreviated *mitte*, meaning 'give this number'.
- The subscription or directions for compounding the drug. This is nowadays usually omitted because most drugs are prepacked and merely require to be dispensed.
- The signature, indicated by the abbreviation *sig*, from the Latin *signa*, meaning 'mark', which indicates to the druggist or pharmacist what instructions should be marked on the medicine for the patient.

Prima luce

'Early in the morning.' In prescription-writing the abbreviation *prim. luc.* could be used to indicate that a drug is to be taken first thing in the morning. Cf. *mane primo*.

Primum non nocere

'First, do no harm.' Many people mistakenly think that this tenet was written by Hippocrates and included in the Hippocratic Oath. It does not appear in the Hippocratic Oath at all. Scholars think that this was a Latin translation of a Greek text, possibly written by Galen. It is, however, a very fine principle for all practitioners of medicine. See *Galen*.

Principiis obsta: sero medicina paratur, cum mala per longas convaluere moras
'Withstand the beginnings; the remedy is prepared too late when, through long delays, diseases have become rooted' – Ovid. See *Ovid*.

Pro dosi
'For one dose only.'

Prognosis
Prediction – from the Greek *pro*, 'before', and the Greek *gnosis*, 'knowledge'. Essentially a prognosis is an attempt to make a prediction on the outcome of a disease, what its course will be, how long it will last and what its ultimate end will be. Hippocrates said that all doctors should practise the art of prognostics. See *diagnosis*.

Pro rationae aetatis
'According to age.' This is a very important issue because children and the elderly have different dose requirements from healthy adults. This prescription *pro. rat. aet* is unlikely to be used nowadays, as the actual amount of a drug should be stated clearly by the prescriber.

Pro re nata
'Take as required.' In writing a prescription one may use the abbreviation *p.r.n.* if a medicine is to be taken when-

ever needed to control a symptom. An analgesic or painkilling drug may be prescribed thus. See *Si opus sit.*

Psittacosis
Parrot fever – from *psittacus*, 'parrot', and the Greek – *osis*, 'a condition'. This is an infectious disease of parrots and related birds such as parakeets and love birds, caused by the bacterium *Chlamydia psittaci*, which is communicable to humans, in whom it produces high fever, severe headache, and symptoms similar to pneumonia. See *chlamydia.*

Pudendal nerve
The main nerve of the perineum and pelvis, responsible for urination, defaecation and orgasm in both sexes – from *pudendus*, meaning 'ashamed'. The term referred to 'the shameful parts' – the genitals. One should not underestimate its importance, however, no matter how ashamed of their pudendal nerves the early anatomists were.

Pulvis
A powder. In prescription-writing the abbreviation *pulv.* could be used to indicate that a medicine must be given in powder form.

Pupil
The apple of the eye, called by the Romans the 'little doll' – from *pupilla*, 'small doll'. The reason for this derivation is that a small person like a tiny doll (a reflection) is seen in the pupil of the eye. This comes about because the eyeball is a spherical organ containing the jelly-like vitreous humor and the fluid aqueous humor. Both of these are transparent. The blackness of the pupil is produced because the interior of the eyeball is in dark-

ness, like the inside of a camera. This being the case, the pupil acts like a tiny mirror to show a reflection of anyone who stands close to the owner of the pupil. The appearance of 'red eyes' when a photograph is taken with a flashlight is caused because the retina at the back of the eye is suddenly illuminated, so reveal the actual colour of the retina with its network of blood vessels.

Pus

White or yellow inflammatory fluid, as found in boils and abscesses – from the Latin word *pus*. Pus is made up of tissue fluid, white blood cells, living and dead bacteria and tissue debris. See *ubi pus, ibi evacua*.

Pyrexia

A fever – from the Greek, *pyrexis*, 'feverishness'. This word has more or less superseded the old word fever in medical texts. Similarly, anti-pyretic has replaced the word febrifuge. See *anti-pyretic, febrifuge* and *fever*.

Q

Quadriceps

Literally, a muscle with four heads – from *quad*, 'four' and *ceps* derived from *caput*, 'head'. The quadriceps is not actually one muscle but a collection of four on the front of the thigh, commonly referred to as the 'quads'. The *rectus femoris* crosses both the hip and knee joint. The other three, *vastus medialis*, *vastus intermedius* and *vastus lateralis* act on the knee joint only. The action of the group of four is to extend the leg and flex the thigh, as when one lifts the leg to step over something and step forward.

Quae prosunt omnibus artes

'The arts which serve everyone'. Motto of the Royal College of Surgeons in England.

Qualis sit animus, ipse animus nescit

'The mind itself does not know what the mind is' – Cicero. See *Cicero*.

Quantum libet

'As much as you like.' In prescription-writing the abbreviation *q.l.* was used to indicate that a medicine could be given or taken in liberal quantity. This would not be used nowadays.

Quantum sufficiat

'A sufficient quantity.' In prescription-writing the abbreviation *q.s.* is used to indicate that a medicine must be supplied in sufficient quantity to last for so long. Nowadays this is not used, since a specific quantity needs to be given.

Quaque die
'Every day.' In prescription-writing, the abbreviation *q.d.* or *qq.d.* may be used to indicate that a medication should be taken once every day.

Quaque hora
'Every hour.' In prescription-writing, the abbreviation *q.h.* may be used to indicate that a medication should be taken once every hour.

Quaque quarta hora
'Every fourth hour.' In prescription-writing the abbreviation *q.q.h.* used to be used to indicate that a medicine must be given every fourth hour.

Quater in die
'Four times a day.' In prescription-writing, the abbreviation *q.i.d.* may be used to indicate that a medication should be taken four times every day, usually at regular, 6-hour, intervals.

Qui docet discit
'He who teaches learns.' The word 'doctor' comes from *docere*, meaning 'to teach'. And as every doctor knows, you are continually learning from your patients.

Quid pro quo
'Something for something.'

Qui medice vivit misere vivit
'Who lives medically lives miserably' – Burton. See *Anatomy of Melancholia*.

Quintilian
Marcus Fabius Quintilianus (AD 30–circa 99) was a famous teacher of rhetoric, who numbered Pliny the Younger among his pupils. He wrote *Institutio oratoria* (the Teaching of Oratory), the textbook of Roman oratory.

Quod cibus est aliis, aliis est venenum
'One man's meat is another man's poison.'

Quod medicina aliis, aliis est acre venenum
'One person's medicine is another's foul poison.' Or, 'One man's meat is another man's poison.' Hence allergies and drug reactions.' See *iatrogenic illness*.

Quod vide
'Which see.' This is used extensively in texts, whereby the abbreviation *q.v.* is used to indicate a cross-reference, where an explanation is given elsewhere in the text.

Quod vespillo facit, fecerat et medicus
'What he is doing as an undertaker, he also used to do as a doctor.' In Roman times doctors were usually freedmen or slaves. They were not always thought of very highly as suggested by this quotation from the satirist Martialis. See *Martial*.

Quotidie
'Daily.' In prescription-writing the abbreviation *quotid.* could be used to indicate that a medicine must be taken daily.

R

Rabies
'The raving disease' – from *rabere*, 'to rave'. A dangerous disease caused by a specific rhabdovirus, transmitted through the saliva of a rabid animal, usually after being bitten. It affects the brain and central nervous system and in its later stages there is increased salivation, unusual behaviour, dehydration and painful spasms of the throat. The latter accounts for the old name of hydrophobia, or fear of water.

Radius
The radial bone – from *radius*, 'a spoke'. This is one of the two bones of the forearm. It is the one on the thumb side. It swings across the ulna whenever you rotate your wrist or hand. It was named by Galen because of its resemblance to the spoke of a wheel. See *Galen*.

Rara avis
'A rare bird.' This is used to indicate an extraordinary or unusually rare occurrence. In modern vernacular a doctor might say that a particular condition is as rare as hen's teeth. The original quote comes from Juvenal's *Satires: rara avis in terris nigroque simillima cycno* – 'a rare bird on the earth, and very like a black swan'.

Recipe

'Take (thou).' In prescription-writing, the abbreviation *Rx* is used to indicate that the patient must take whatever is prescribed. This is a universal sign of a prescription and is found in doctors' notes and often on the top of prescriptions. See *prescription*.

Rectum

The straight lower part of the large bowel, terminating in the anus – from *rectus*, meaning 'straight'. Galen (circa AD 129–200) described the rectum and gave it the name, because in dissections of other animals he had found it to be straight. See *Galen*.

Rectus

Straight muscle – from *rectus*, 'straight'. These muscles have fairly direct actions. *Rectus* muscles that are involved in eye movements are *superior rectus*, *inferior rectus*, *lateral rectus* and *medial rectus*. They are attached around the orbital or eyeball axis and control the up, down and side-to-side movements of the eyeball.

Rectus abdominis

The straight muscle of the abdomen – from *rectus*, 'straight' and *abdominus*, meaning 'of the abdomen'. This is essentially the flat muscle of the tummy or the six-pack muscle. Everyone has one, it is just that many people have theirs well hidden.

Rectus femoris

Straight muscle of the thigh – from *rectus*, 'straight' and *femoris*, 'to do with the femur or thigh bone'. This muscle has its origin on the pelvis, then stretches flat across the thigh and crosses the patella or knee-cap, to be inserted into the tibia, or upper part of the shin. It helps to flex the hip and straighten the knee. Footballers cannot do without it.

Reflex

An action that is directed backwards – from *reflexus*, 'go back'. There are many reflexes in the body, both of the muscles and of the inner organs. The *knee jerk reflex* occurs when the patellar tendon is struck, since a loop causes the quadriceps muscle to contract. The *gastro-colic reflex* occurs whenever food enters the stomach, causing the lower bowel, the colon to start making room and moving its contents further down. And artificial conditioned reflexes can occur, as were proven by Ivan Pavlov and his salivating Alsatian dog.

Reflexology

Literally the study of reflexes – from *reflexus*, 'go back' and the Greek *logos*, 'the study of something'. Reflexology is a complementary therapy. In 1913 Dr William Fitzgerald introduced this therapy to the West as 'zone therapy'. He noted that reflex areas on the feet and hands were linked to other areas and organs of the body within the same zone. In the 1930s Eunice Ingham further developed this into what is now known as reflexology. She observed that congestion or tension in any part of the foot is mirrored in the corresponding part of the body. According to reflexologists, by working on the reflexes of the feet one can bring healing to the part of the body that is unwell.

Renal

'Of the kidney' – from *renalis*, 'of a kidney', itself derived from *ren*, 'kidney'.

Renal calculus
A kidney stone – from *renalis*, 'of a kidney' and *calculus*, 'pebble or stone'.

Renal cortex
The outer part of the kidney – from *renalis*, 'of the kidney' and *cortex*, 'tree bark'. The renal cortex contains the glomeruli, the filtering parts of the kidney.

Renal medulla
The inner part of the kidney, which controls mineral exchange and drains into the renal pelvis – from *renalis*, 'of the kidney', and *medulla*, 'middle part'.

Renal pelvis
The collecting part of the kidney, which drains directly into the ureter – from *renalis*, 'of the kidney', and *pelvis*, 'basin'.

Repetatur
'Let it be repeated.' In prescription-writing the abbreviation *rept.* is used to indicate that a medicine or course of medication can be repeated.

Requiescat in pace
'Rest in peace' – often abbreviated to *RIP.*

Res in cardine est
'The next 24 hours will tell.' The case is critical and has to be taken a day at a time.

Retina
The net at the back of the eye – from *rete*, 'net'. The retina is the thin layer at the back of the eye which contains the rods and cones, the sensitive receptors that allow us to

perceive light and colour. Interestingly, there is no actual net-like structure in the retina, so it is a bit of a misnomer. The name probably comes about because of the way in which the word was translated. Galen used the Greek word *amphiblestron* to describe it. This word has two meanings – a fisherman's coat and a fisherman's net. It is believed that Galen used the word in the first sense, but when it was translated into Latin, the translator incorrectly chose the second meaning.

Rhinitis medicamentosa
Inflammation of the lining of the nose as the result of too much treatment – from the Greek *rhinos*, 'nose', and *-itis*, 'inflammation of', and *medicamentosa*, from *medicare*, 'to heal' and *osa*, corruption of *-osis*, 'illness of'. See *iatrogenic illness*.

Rhinoplasty
A 'nose job' operation – from the Greek words *rhinos* and *plastia*, meaning 'nose' and 'shaping'.

Rigor mortis
'Rigidness or stiffness of death.' Rigor mortis is the state a body reaches when the oxygen supply to the muscles ceases but the cells continue to respire. In the absence of oxygen lactic acid builds up, which causes the muscles to stiffen. The body will become stiff after about three hours and remain that way for around 36 hours. When the cells all die then rigor mortis ceases.

Risorius
The grinning muscle – from *risor*, meaning 'scoffer'. This muscle attaches to the obicularis oris and pulls the mouth sidewards, to stretch it into a grin.

Risus sardonicus

'A fixed or sardonic grin.' This is a medical term indicating a painful spasm of the facial muscles, usually as a result of tetanus. The mouth is pulled into a fixed grin. It is also used to refer to neurotic or uncontrolled (inappropriate) laughter with a fixed grin.

S

Sacral plexus
The main nerve network for the lower limb – literally the braid of the holy bone, from *sacrum*, 'sacred, holy', and *plexus*, 'braid'. See *plexus*.

Sacrum
Actually, *os sacrum* – the holy bone – from *os*, 'bone', and *sacrum*, 'sacred, holy'. The sacrum is the large bone at the base of the spine, which acts as the anchor for the pelvis. The sacrum actually consists of five fused sacral vertebrae.

Salerno School of Health
The earliest Italian medical school opened in Salerno in the ninth century, and as the place where the streams of classical, Arab and Jewish medicine flowed together it was the predecessor of the medical renaissance. It reached its height of influence in the twelfth century. A number of medical texts have survived from the Salerno School on various aspects of medicine, the best known being the *Regimen Sanitatis Salernitanum*, the *Salerno Book of Health*. The book is filled with axioms and maxims for maintaining health, at a time when medicine was largely ineffective. It was translated by Sir John Harington, the inventor of the so-called seat of civilization, the water closet.

Saliva
Saliva – from the Latin word for 'spit'. Saliva is a clear liquid that is produced by the salivary glands (parotid,

submandibular and sublingual) and secreted into the mouth twenty-four hours a day. Throughout the day between one to two litres are produced. This fluid lubricates food to ease swallowing and helps the tongue with the sense of taste. It also contains enzymes which begin the process of digestion while food is still in the mouth. Saliva has also been shown to contain inorganic nitrites which react with the skin to produce nitric oxide, a chemical that can kill bacteria. This, together with the discovery of a protein called *secretory leukocyte protease inhibitor* (SLPI), which has been demonstrated to enhance skin healing, confirms the old observation that licked wounds heal faster.

Sapientia manaque apta
'Wisdom and a skilful hand.' Motto of the Canadian Association of General Surgeons.

Sartorius muscle
The tailor's muscle, from *sartor*, 'tailor'. This muscle arises from the outside of the hip and crosses to the inside of the knee. It works to bend and cross the leg; the position that tailors used in days gone by. Yoga adepts use it when adopting the lotus position.

Scalpel
Surgeon's knife – from *scalpellum*, meaning 'small carving knife'. A scalpel is a surgical knife, with a single-edged cutting blade. Often the blades are detachable and can be applied to the handles before the surgical procedure. Sometimes the word lancet is confused with scalpel, but a lancet is a two-edged blade used for making punctures in the skin, generally in order to obtain a small sample of blood.

Scapula
'The shoulder-blade', from the Latin word *scapula*.

Scatula
'A box'. In prescription-writing the abbreviation *scat* would indicate that a box of a particular medication should be dispensed.

Scientia potestas est
'Knowledge is power' – Francis Bacon. See *Bacon*.

Scrotum
The pouch that contains the testicles – from *scroteus*, 'leather pouch'. The scrotum does indeed resemble a leather pouch, because it is capable of wrinkling when it is cold. This is in fact a defence mechanism, since the function of the scrotum is to keep its contents, the testes, at a constant temperature that is slightly lower than that of the rest of the body. This temperature is around 34.4 °C, whereas the average body temperature is 36.7 °C, a temperature that may be too high for the production of sperm. Two muscles control the temperature of the scrotum. The cremaster muscle in the abdomen draws the testes upwards when it is cold, at the same time as the dartos muscle under the scrotal skin, which contracts to warm the testes. When it is warm the muscles relax to allow cooling.

Secundum artem
'According to custom.' In prescription-writing the abbreviation *sec. art.* used to be used to indicate that a medicine should be taken in the usual manner. This is too nebulous a prescription to be used nowadays.

Secundis horis
'Every two hours.' In prescription-writing the abbreviation *sec. hor.* could be used to indicate that a medicine must be taken every two hours.

Sella turcica
The Turkish Saddle, from *sella*, 'saddle', and *turcica*, 'Turkish'. A saddle-shaped part of the sphenoid bone inside the skull. The pituitary gland sits in the saddle like a rider. See *pituitary gland*.

Semimembranosus
One of the three hamstring muscles, together with *biceps femoris* and *semitendinosus*. These muscles help to straighten the leg at the hip and bend the leg at the knee. Understandably, runners and athletes often pull (strain) them. The upper half of the semimembranosus is membranous – from *semi*, 'half', and *membrana*, 'membrane'. See *biceps femoris* and *semitendinosus*.

Seminiferous tubules
The testicular sperm tubes – from *semen*, 'seed', and *ferre*, 'to carry, to bear'.

Semitendinosus
One of the three hamstring muscles, together with *biceps femoris* and *semimembranosus*. These muscles help to straighten the leg at the hip and bend the leg at the knee. The lower half of the semitendinosus is tendon. From *semi*, 'half' and *tendo*, 'I stretch, sinew'. See *biceps femoris* and *semimembranosus*.

Seneca
Lucius Annaeus Seneca (circa 5 BCE–AD 65), known as Seneca the Younger (his father, known as the Elder had

been a respected teacher of rhetoric) was a Stoic, writer and laywer. He was famous for his philosophical treatise, the *Epistulae morales*, a series of 124 essays on Stoic philosophy. He had been banished from Rome by the Emperor Claudius on a charge of adultery with Julia Livilla, the emperor's niece. He was later allowed to return as the future Emperor Nero's tutor. A true Stoic, he committed suicide upon Nero's order.

Serratus anterior

The saw muscle of the chest – from *serra*, meaning 'saw', and *anterior* indicating the 'front'. This saw-shaped muscle connects the ribs with the scapula or shoulder blade. It is the main muscle that pulls the scapula forward when you push.

Sesamoid bones

Bones that resemble 'sesame' seeds. This term is used in anatomy to describe bones that form within certain tendons, where they rub on convex body surfaces. They are generally very small and of little significance, but seem to develop to reduce pressure. Galen described them as being like sesame seeds. The largest of them is, however, very significant, for it is the kneecap or patella. See *patella*.

Sesquipedalian

A polysyllabic word – from *sesqui*, 'one-and-a-half', and *pes*, 'foot'. The Roman writer Horace introduced this word in his *Ars Poetica (The Art of Poetry): Proicit ampullas et sesquipedalia verba*, which means 'He throws aside his paint pots and his words that are a foot-and-a-half long.' Doctors have always been excessively fond of the longest words possible, as witnessed in this book. The cynic might suggest that if you want to disguise the fact that you don't know how a condition occurs, how it will continue and how on earth you can cure it, you give it a very long Latin name. Surprisingly, dermatology seems to have the greatest number of sesquipedalian diagnoses.

Sextus horis
'Every six hours.' In prescription-writing the abbreviation *sex. hor.* could be used to indicate that a medicine must be taken every six hours.

Sic
'Thus.'

Sic quibus intumuit suffuse venter ab unda; quo plus sunt potae plus sitiuntur aquae
'So with those who are swollen with dropsy, the more water they drink the more they thirst' – Ovid. An astute observation that people in severe heart failure are unable to maintain their fluid balance. See *Ovid*.

Signa, signetur
'Label, let it be labelled.' In prescription-writing the abbreviation *sig.* is used to indicate that a medicine must be according to the following instructions. See *prescription*.

Similia similibus curentur
'Let likes be treated by likes.' This is the guiding principle of homoeopathic medicine. It was first set down by Samuel Hahnemann. It is the principle that a condition can be treated by giving a small amount (infinitesimal sometimes) of a substance, which, if given in a pure form could produce those same symptoms. It works by essen-

tially stimulating the body to regulate itself. This principle is often misquoted, even in homoeopathic texts as 'similia similibus *curantur*'. This gives the meaning 'like will be cured by like', which is incorrect. See *contraria contrariis curantur* and *homoeopathy*.

Si opus sit
'Give or take if needed.' In prescription-writing the abbreviation *s.o.s.* could be used when a remedy is to be used as necessary. See *pro re nata*.

Sine
'Without.' In prescription-writing the word *sine* would be used to indicate that a medicine must be given without a particular ingredient.

Sine mora
'Without delay.'

Sine prole
'Without children.'

Sine qua non
Literally, 'without which not'. This means that something is absolutely necessary.

Sinus
'A hollow', from the Latin *sinus*. In anatomy this refers to any hollow or cavity. The facial sinuses are chambers or cavities within the facial bones around the eyes and the nose. *Sinusitis* is the name for the condition in which there is inflammation of the facial sinuses. The word also refers to a pathological channel that may form as pus tracks through tissue from an abscess.

Si tibi deficiant medici, medici tibi fiant haec tria, mens hilaris, requies, moderata dieta

'If doctors fail you, let these three be your doctors; a cheerful mind, rest and moderate diet' – maxim of the Salerno School of Health. See *Salerno School of Health*.

Solar Plexus

A complex anatomical network, literally 'the sun's braid' – from *solaris*, 'of the sun', and *plexus*, 'braid'. More correctly, this is the coeliac plexus, a network of nerves in the upper abdomen that spreads out like the rays of the sun. It is the target for boxers when trying to wind an opponent. See *coeliac* and *plexus*.

Sphincter

A circular closing muscle – from the Greek *sphigkter*, 'the squeezer'. The Greek sphinx of Thebes was a monster with a woman's head and bust, a lion's body, and the wings of an eagle. Travellers on the road to ancient Thebes who failed to answer her riddle were squeezed to death and then devoured. Only Oedipus was able to rise to the challenge. (See *Oedipus*). A sphincter is a circular muscle that, when it contracts, closes an orifice or opening. For example, the anal sphincters (there are internal and external ones) close the anus and lower rectum, the sphincter of Boyden closes the common bile duct, the sphincter of Oddi closes the bile and pancreatic ducts, the cardiac or gastroeosophageal sphincter closes off the gullet from the stomach, the pyloric sphincter closes the stomach from the duodenum and the pupillary sphincter constricts the pupil of the eye. In addition, another large muscle with a sphincter-like action is the *orbicularis oris*, the ring muscle that lies within the lips and surrounds the mouth, and closes the mouth in a pouting fashion. There is also the *orbicularis oculi*, which surrounds each eye, and screws it closed to produce the little 'crow's foot' wrinkles outside the eye. See *orbicularis oculi* and *orbicularis oris*.

Stapes
Ear stirrup – from *stapes*, 'stirrup'. One of the ossicles of the middle ear. See *ossicles*.

Staphylococcus
Grape-shaped bacteria – from the Greek *staphylos*, 'bunch of grapes', and *kokkos*, 'berry'. Many of the Staphylococcus group live on the human skin without causing any problem. *Staphylococcus aureus* is the one most likely to cause an infection, abscess or carbuncle. At one time penicillin would deal with this organism but many of them have developed resistance to antibiotics. Now society has a problem with the so-called hospital superbug, methicillin resistant staphylococcus aureus (MRSA). It is believed that overuse of antibiotics is allowing these micro-organisms to evolve. They are in fact merely developing means of living in a hazardous and dangerous environment, since antibiotics are dangerous to their health. See *bacteria*.

Statim
'Immediately.' In prescription-writing the abbreviation *stat.* is used to indicate that a medicine must be taken immediately.

Sternocleidomastoid
The large muscle of the neck – from *sternum*, 'breast bone', the Greek *kleidos*, meaning 'clavicle', and *mastos*, 'breast' and *oid*, 'shaped like'. This large muscle joins the

breast bone, the clavicle and the mastoid process behind the ear. It is the big muscle that turns your head to the side. See *sternum*, *clavicle* and *mastoid bone*.

Sternum

The breast bone – from the Late Latin word *sternum* meaning 'breast bone'. In fact, before the word sternum was coined, the breast bone was likened to a gladiator's sword, for it has three distinct pieces. These are:

- *Manubrium* – the handle of the sword, from the Latin, meaning 'handle'.
- *Gladiolus* – the body of the sternum, from the Latin word for a 'short sword'.
- *Xiphoid process* – the tip of the sword, from the Greek words *xiphos*, meaning 'sword' and *-oid*, 'like'.

Stethoscope

Almost the doctor's badge of office, the stethoscope consists of the listening tubes for sounding the heart and lungs. Its name comes from the Greek words, *stethos*, 'chest' and *skopos*, 'watcher'. It is, literally, the instrument to watch or examine the chest (although it is a listening device in fact). The first stethoscope was a simple rolled-up tube of paper, used by the French physician René Laennec. After discovering that he could hear different sounds in patients' chests with a simple listening device like this he spent three years perfecting his design for an improved version. Basically, he correlated his chest findings on patients with pneumonia and compared what he heard to their autopsy findings. From this he published the first seminal work on the use of listening to body sounds entitled *De L'auscultation mediate* in 1819. The modern stethoscope, the 'two-ear' type, was invented in

1852 by the American physician George Cammann. The use of the stethoscope is a skill that takes medical students several years to master. My cynical old professor of medicine used to call them 'guessing tubes'.

Stratum
Layer – from *stratus*, 'flat layer'. The skin is the largest and heaviest organ in the body, accounting for sixteen per cent of the body weight. It is composed of a series of layers:

Stratum corneum
The horny layer – from *stratus*, 'layer', and *cornu*, 'horn'. This is the outermost horny layer, which is thickest on the palms of the hands and the soles of the feet. It has a build-up of keratin in its cells. Insensitive folk may be said to have a deeper stratum corneum than others (which isn't true!). See *keratin*.

Stratum germinativum
The growing layer – from *stratus*, 'layer', and *germinativum*, 'growing'. This is a deeper layer where new cells are produced.

Stratum lucidum
The see-through layer – from *stratus*, 'layer', and *lucidum*, 'clear'. This is just below the stratum corneum.

Streptococcus
Twisted rows of berry-shaped bacteria – from the Greek *streptos*, 'twisted', and *kokkos*, 'berry'. These bacteria cause all sorts of infection in humans. *Streptococcus pyogenes* is particularly important because it can cause tonsillitis, erysipelas, wound infections and septicaemia.

Sub
'Under, below.'

Subinde
'Frequently.' In prescription-writing the abbreviation *subind.* could be used to indicate that a medicine may be taken frequently, as needed.

Sub lingua
'Under the tongue.' In writing a prescription, the abbreviation SL would be used, to indicate that a spray was to be squirted sublingually, under the tongue, or in the case of a tablet that it should be dissolved under the tongue.

Super ardua
'Let us overcome our difficulties.' Motto of the Royal College of Obstetricians and Gynaecologists.

Supervacuus inter sanos medicus
'The physician is superfluous among the healthy' – Tacitus. See *Tacitus*.

Suppositorium
A pellet to be inserted in the rectum. In prescription-writing the abbreviation *supp.* could be used to indicate that a drug is to be issued as a suppository. See *per rectum*.

Supra
'Above or over.'

Supratentorial
Literally 'above the tent'. This is one of those occult terms used by doctors when discussing a problem that

may be psychological or psychosomatic in origin, rather than physical. It refers to the *tentorium cerebri*, a tentlike membrane that separates the cerebellum of the brain from the cerebrum. The cerebrum is where all the thinking takes place, so to say that something is supra-tentorial is to say that it is psychological.

Symphysis pubis

Where the two pubic bones meet – from the Latin *pubes*, meaning 'grown up, adult', and the Greek words *sym*, 'with, or together', and *physis*, 'growing'.

Symptom

A feeling that something is not right – a subjective aware-ness of a manifestation of illness or disease. For example a cough, a pain, feeling hot, cold or nauseated. It comes from the Greek *sym*, 'with' and the Greek *ptoma*, 'calamity or disease'. In other words the feelings that come with disease. This distinguishes it from a *sign* of disease, such as a rash, a heart murmur, or the presence of jaundice.

Syncope

A faint – from the Greek *syn*, 'with', and the Greek *kope*, 'cutting'. Hence it means 'cut short'. A faint or loss of consciousness occurs there is a shortage of blood to the brain, from one of many causes. *Cardiogenic syncope* is the name for a faint occurring as the result of some acute problem with the heart. *Micturition syncope* is the name for a faint while passing urine. And *vasovagal syncope* is the general name for a faint due to stimula-tion of the blood vessels and the vagus nerve, causing the heart to beat slowly and the blood pressure to drop dramatically.

Syrus, Publilius

Publilius Syrus was a writer of mimes in the first century BCE. He was a native of Syria, who had been brought to Rome as a slave, hence his name, it being common to name slaves after their place of origin. Because of his wit and obvious talent, his master gave him his freedom and educated him. Publilius was perhaps even more famous as an *improvisatore*, and received from Caesar himself the prize in a contest of wit in which he vanquished all his competitors. All that remains of his works is a collection of *Sentences* (*Sententiae*), a series of moral maxims.

T

Tabella
'A tablet.' In prescription-writing the abbreviation *tab.* is used to indicate that a medicine must be dispensed in tablet form.

Tabula rasa
'A blank slate.' The Romans used to write on wax tablets, which were easy to erase. Literally, *tabula rasa* means a scraped (clean) slate. John Locke, Oxford scholar, philosopher and physician (1632–1704) said that this was like the human mind at birth, before it acquires any knowledge.

Tachycardia
A racing heart – from the Greek *tachys*, 'fast, swift', and *kardos*, 'heart'.

Tacitus
Gaius Cornelius Tacitus (AD 56–117), Roman orator, lawyer, and senator, is considered one of antiquity's greatest historians. His major works – *Annales* (the *Annals*) and *Historiae* (the *Histories*) – covered the history of the Roman Empire's first century, from the accession of the Emperor Tiberius to the death of Domitian.

Taenia saginata
The beef tapeworm – from *taenia*, 'ribbon'. Among the Egyptian medical papyri, the Ebers papyrus refers to

tapeworms, and these records can be confirmed by the discovery of calcified tapeworm eggs in mummies dating from 1200 BCE. The adult tapeworm can reach a length of up to eight metres. It is contracted from eating infected meat. *Taenia solium*, the pork tapeworm, is rarely contracted from eating infected pork. Both are rare in the developed world.

Talipes
Club foot – from *talus*, 'ankle' and *pes*, 'foot'. This is a congenital abnormality of the foot and ankle.

Talipes equino-varus is the commonest type of clubfoot, in which the foot is bent inwards (*varus*) and the individual walks on the tips of his toes, like a horse (from *equines*).

Talipes calcaneo-valgus is a less common type of clubfoot, in which the individual walks on his heel (*calcaneo*) and the foot is bent outwards (*valgus*). The Emperor Claudius suffered from Talipes deformity.

Tardiora sunt remedia quam mala
'Remedies are slower than illness' – Tacitus. See *Tacitus*.

Tempore ducetur longo fortasse cicatrix; horrent admotas vulnera cruda manus
'A wound will perhaps become tolerable with length of time; but wounds which are raw shudder at the touch of the hands' – Ovid. See *Ovid*.

Temporis ars medicina fere est
'The art of medicine is generally a question of time' – Ovid. Essentially, time is a great healer. See *Ovid*.

Tempus fugit
'Time flies.'

Tendo calcaneus
The sinew of the heel, from *tendo*, 'sinew', or 'stretched cord', and 'of the heel'. Also known as *Achilles tendon*, because legend tells us that the great Greek hero was dipped in the magical water of the River Styx by his mother to make him invulnerable. She held him by the foot, so his heel was not immersed and his heel was to prove his weak spot. At the battle of Troy, after Achilles slew Hector, Paris avenged his brother's death by shooting a poisoned arrow into Achilles's unprotected heel. This is the sinew that attaches the calf muscles – the gastrocnemis and soleus muscles (*triceps surae*) to the back of the calcaneus, or heel bone.

Tendon
A sinew – from *tendo*, 'sinew' or 'cord'. A tendon attaches a muscle to a bone.

Ter die sumendus
'To be taken three times a day.' In prescription-writing the abbreviation *t.d.s.* is used to indicate that a medicine must be taken three times a day.

Terence
Publius Terentius Afer (190 BCE–159 BCE), was a popular comic playwright who came to Rome as a slave from Africa, hence his name, Afer, it being common to name slaves after their place of origin. All six of his comedies survive. He was accused of plagiarizing the Greek dramatist Menander. His reply was that 'nothing has ever been said that has not been said before.'

Ter in die

'Three times a day.' In prescription-writing the abbreviation *t.i.d.* is used to indicate that a medicine must be taken three times a day.

Ter quaterve die

'Three or four times a day.' In prescription-writing the abbreviation *t.q.d.* could be used to indicate that a medicine must be taken three or four times a day.

Terra salutiferas herbas, eademque nocentes nutrit, et urticae proxima, saepe rosa est

'The same earth nourishes health-giving and injurious plants, and the rose is often close to the nettle' – Ovid. Take care when giving medicine, for you never quite know if one will have a side effect! See *Ovid*.

Testis and testicle

The male genital organ – from *testis*, 'witness'. The origin of the name for this organ may seem obscure to us today. Yet in Roman times only a man could 'testify' in court, or appear as a witness. Women and eunuchs were excluded, so the presence of testes (plural of testis) was proof of being a man. So, testicles are a man's 'little witnesses'.

Thorax

The chest – from the Greek *thorakis*, an 'armoured breast-plate'. The thorax is the large chamber of the chest that extends from the neck to the diaphragm, excluding the upper limbs. It contains the heart and lungs and is protected by the bony ribcage, consisting of the ribs and sternum, or breastbone.

Thyroid

The door-shaped shield – from the Greek *thyreo-eides*. In Ancient Greece a *thyreos* was a door-shaped shield with a notch for the chin, from *thyra*, 'door'. The thyroid is a gland on the front of the neck, which produces thyroxine, the thyroid hormone. This controls the rate of metabolism in the body. Underactivity (hypothyroidism or myxoedema) causes sluggishness and weight gain, whereas over-activity (hyperthyroidism or Graves' disease) causes palpitations, anxiety and weight loss.

Tibia

The large lower leg bone – from *tibia*, meaning 'a flute'. In Roman days musicians used the tibias of animals and birds to make pipes and flutes.

Timor mortis morte pejor

'The fear of death is worse than death' – Burton. See the *Anatomy of Melancholy*.

Tinctura

'A tincture' – a medicinal solution of a substance, often of vegetable origin, in which alcohol, an alcohol-water mixture, glycerine or sodium chloride solution is used as a solvent. In prescription-writing the abbreviation *tinct.* could be used to indicate that a medicine must be dispensed in tincture form.

Tinctura cardamomi compositae

A mixture of cardamom, caraway, cochineal, glycerin and alcohol; a placebo, formerly used as a 'tonic' and as a mild carminative. See *carminative* and *placebo*.

Tinctura cinchonae compositae

A mixture of quinine, orange peel, serpentary, cochineal and alcohol, a placebo, formerly used as a 'tonic' and a remedy for rheumatism. See *placebo*.

Tinea

A fungal skin infection – from *tinea*, 'moth-eaten'. Doctors describe various types of tineal infection, depending upon which part of the body is affected. Hence:

Tinea capitis – fungal infection of the scalp.

Tinea corporis – fungal infection of the trunk.

Tinea pedis – fungal infection of the foot, or good old athlete's foot.

Tolle causam

'Seek the cause.' A basic principle in medicine. Motto of the Institute of Psionic Medicine.

Tollere nodosam nescit medicina podagram

'Medicine does not know how to remove the nodous (knotty) gout' – Ovid. See *Ovid* and *opprobrium medicorum*.

Torticollis

A wry neck – from *tortus*, 'twisted' and *collum*, 'neck'. This is due to spasm of the *sternocleidomastoid* muscle. See *sternocleidomastoid*.

Triceps

The three-headed muscle, from *tres*, 'three', and *ceps*, derived from *caput*, 'head'. The large muscle on the back of the upper arm, which extends or straightens the arm.

The three heads refer to its three points of origin, one on the scapula or shoulder blade and two on the humerus or upper arm bone. Its tendon is attached to the olecranon of the radius bone.

Triceps surae
The three-headed muscle of the calf, from *tres*, 'three', *ceps*, 'head', and *sura*, 'calf'. The two bellies of the *gastrocnemius* muscle give the calf its fullness, and the *soleus*, shaped like a boot sole, gives strength to the Achilles tendon.

Trochiscus
'A lozenge.' In prescription-writing the abbreviation *troch.* could be used to indicate that lozenges must be dispensed.

Tumour
A growth – from the Latin *tumor*, 'swelling'. This was originally used to mean swelling, one of the four cardinal signs of swelling as described by Celsus – *calor* (warmth), *dolor* (pain), *rubor* (redness) and *tumor* (swelling). Nowadays a tumour refers to an overgrowth of tissue, or a growth of some sort. These can be either benign or malignant. See *Celsus*.

Tussi urgente
'When the cough is troublesome.' In prescription-writing the abbreviation *tuss. urg.* could be used to indicate that a linctus or cough remedy should be taken when a cough is particularly troublesome.

U

Ubi pus, ibi evacua
'Where there is pus, let it out.' This is one of the oldest surgical maxims.

Ubi tres medici, duo athei
'Where there are three doctors, there are two atheists' – Medieval saying.

Ulcer
'Sore' – from the Latin *ulcus*. Ulcers are open sores that can occur on the skin, on the surface of the eyeball and on mucous membranes in any part of the body. Wherever they occur they tend to produce intense pain.

Ulcerative colitis
An inflammatory condition of the colon, characterized by patches of ulceration of its lining. See *colon*.

Ulna
Elbow – from *ulna*, meaning 'elbow'. The ulna is the larger of the two bones of the forearm, the other being the radius.

Ultra
'Above.' Hence ultrasonic means above sound, ultra-violet means above the violet light of the spectrum.

Umbilicus

'Navel.' The umbilicus is the navel or belly-button. It is the vestige of the point where the umbilical cord attached the baby to the placenta during intrauterine life.

Unguentum

'An ointment.' In prescription-writing the abbreviation *ung.* is used to indicate that a particular ointment is to be dispensed.

Unilateral

One-sided – from *unus*, 'one', and *lateralus*, 'of the side'. The term is used to indicate when a condition affects one side of the body, for instance shingles or a stroke.

Ureter

The urine tube that carries urine from the kidneys to the bladder – from the Greek *oureter*, 'urine carrier'.

Ureterolithotomy

The operation to remove a stone from the ureter, to relieve renal or ureteric colic – from the Greek *oureter*, 'urine carrier', and the Greek *litho*, 'stone' or 'pebble', and -*otomy*, removal by making a hole into the ureter.

Urethra

The urine tube from the bladder to the exterior – from the Greek *ourethra*, 'urine doorway'.

Urine

Urine, the excreted fluid from the urinary tract – from *urina*, 'urine'. Urine is excreted by the kidneys, passed down the ureters to the bladder, then passed outside the body via the urethra. It is used to remove chemicals and drugs from the body and to maintain the correct fluid balance of the body. When the individual is well hydrated the urine is clear, but when one is dehydrated it becomes concentrated and straw coloured or even orange. It contains salts, minerals and various waste products of metabolism. It is the principal route for excreting alcohol and its breakdown products from the body, and in the medical condition diabetes mellitus it contains sugar. See *Diabetes mellitus*. A subject that has stimulated much research is the phenomenon of 'asparagus urine'. Apparently, 50 per cent of people are able to detect a 'rotting cabbage' odour in their urine after eating asparagus. All sorts of theories abounded as to its significance and a considerable number of investigations have been made over the years. Asparagus is rich in a sulphur-containing substance called mercaptan, which is broken down by the digestive system into odoriferous chemicals which are excreted into the urine within thirty minutes. The most recent research indicates that everyone does actually break this down, but that only 50 per cent of people are able to smell it. They not only smell it in their own urine, but in that of other people who have eaten asparagus. It makes for an interesting after-dinner discussion. Urine is used in various alternative medical systems both externally and internally (by drinking) in the treatment of some conditions.

Usque ad nauseam
'Even to the point of inducing nausea.' See *ad nauseam*.

Ut dictum
'As directed.' In prescription-writing the abbreviation *ut dict.* could be used to indicate that a medicine must be as directed by the doctor.

Utendus

'To be used.' In prescription-writing the abbreviation *utend.* is used to indicate that something is 'to be used' in a particular manner, or a particular number of times, by following it with another abbreviation. For example: *utend. b.d.* – to be used twice a day.

Uterus

Womb – from *uter*, 'bag of goatskin.' Wine and water were carried in goatskin bags in Roman times. The female organ resembles one.

Ut omnes videant

'So that all may see.' Motto of the Royal College of Ophthalmologists.

Uvea

The pigmented layer inside the eye, including the iris – from *uva*, 'grape'. This was first described by the Roman physician Galen. See *Galen*.

Uvula

The 'dangly' lump of flesh at the back of the throat – from *uva*, 'grape' and its diminutive form – *ula* – hence uvula means 'small grape'.

V

Vade mecum
'Go with me' – a vade-mecum is a booklet or small reference work that can be carried about conveniently. Student doctors carry a vade-mecum of drugs, diagnostic signs, appropriate laboratory tests and treatment regimes, around in their bags or pockets.

Vagina
The female front passage that has the uterus or womb at its apex – from the Latin word *vagina*, meaning 'sheath'. In Roman days a *gladius*, the name for a short sword, was a euphemism for a penis. Draw your own conclusions as to how these explanations fit together.

Vaginae synoviales
These have nothing whatever to do with the female vagina, but are the lubricating sheaths that surround some of the tendons of the hands and feet.

Vagus
The tenth cranial nerve. In New Latin *vagus nervus* means 'the wandering nerve'. This is because it has a long course and distribution, extending from the brain medulla down to supply many of the internal organs. See *vasovagal syncope*.

Valetudinarian
A sickly or weak person, who is always concerned about his or her health; a hypochondriac – from *valetudinarius*, itself from *valetudo*, 'state of health'.

Valetudinarium
'A (Roman) hospital.'

Vas deferens
The ducts that carry sperm – from *vas*, 'duct', and *deferens*, 'carrying away'. The sperm ducts.

Vasectomy
Surgical male sterilization, involving cutting and ligating the *vas deferens* in the scrotum.

Vasovagal syncope
The usual type of faint – from *vas*, 'vessel' or 'duct', and *vagal*, appertaining to the vagus nerve and *syncope*. See *syncope*.

Vein
A vein, a blood vessel that carries blood back towards the heart – from *vena*, 'vein'. In general veins are the blood vessels that carry de-oxygenated blood back from the tissues to the right side of the heart, with two main exceptions. The pulmonary veins carry oxygenated blood back from the lungs to the left side of the heart, which then pumps it to the rest of the body. The portal vein transports blood rich in digested products from the intestines to the liver. Veins differ from arteries, which carry blood away from the heart to the tissues, in that they have one-way valves along their length. These prevent blood from flowing backwards

during the moments when the heart fills up between heartbeats.

Vena cava
The empty vein – from the Latin *vena*, 'vein', and *cava*, 'empty'. The two vena cavae – inferior and superior vena cava, are the two large veins that bring blood back to the heart (the inferior from the bottom half of the body and the superior from the upper half). The name refers to the fact that anatomists used to find the veins to be empty after death.

Venereal
Meaning 'to do with sexual contact', hence venereal disease. It refers to Venus, goddess of love.

Verbum sat sapienti
'A word to the wise.'

Vermiform appendix
The worm-like hanger on – from *vermis*, 'worm', *ap*, 'to', and *pendix*, 'hanging part'. In human anatomy, the vermiform appendix (or appendix) is a blind-ended tube connected to the caecum. It develops embryologically from the caecum. In adults, the appendix averages 10 cm in length but can range from 2cm to 20cm. It is situated in the lower right quadrant of the abdomen. We no longer need the appendix. If it becomes inflamed, it is removed surgically in order to prevent the dangerous condition of peritonitis. See *appendicectomy*.

Vermifuge
A drug or agent that will eliminate worms from the body – from *vermis*, 'worm', and *fugere*, 'to flee' (to drive

away). Pumpkin seeds are traditional vermifuges. Interestingly, they are also a good example of the doctrine of signatures in that pumpkin seeds resemble the segments of the tapeworm. Nowadays, there are effective drugs that do the task, mostly combined with laxatives, to help the passage of the worm from the body.

Verruca

A wart, from the Latin *verruca*, meaning 'wart'.

Vertebra

One of the bones of the spine – from the Latin word *vertebra*, meaning 'pivot'. There are thirty-three bones of the spine, seven cervical or neck bones, twelve thoracic or chest vertebra, five lumbar or small of back, five sacral and four coccygeal. The sacral and coccygeal vertebrae are fused to form the *os sacrum* and the *coccyx*. See *sacrum* and *coccyx*.

Vesalius

Andreas Vesalius (AD 1514–64) was a Flemish anatomist who changed the very nature of medical education by bringing the students close to the operating table. He demonstrated that, in many instances, Galen and other early anatomists had been incorrect in some of their assertions (and indeed, he was convinced that Galen had never actually dissected a human). For example, he demonstrated that the heart had four chambers. He conducted his own dissections, and made many discoveries of far-reaching importance. Yet it was his writing that was to give him his place in medical history. In 1543 he wrote the first anatomically accurate medical textbook, *De Humani Corporis Fabrica* (On the Fabric of the Human Body), which was complete with precise illustrations. In 1544 he was appointed court physician to the Emperor Charles V. From then until the emperor's abdication, in 1556, Vesalius accompanied Charles on all his journeys and campaigns. Then he entered the service of King Philip II of Spain. In the spring of 1564 he undertook a pilgrimage to the Holy Land, from which he never returned.

Vestibule
In anatomical terms, an entrance chamber or cavity leading into another chamber or cavity – from *vestibulum*, meaning 'courtyard'. There are anatomical vestibules in the larynx, mouth, nose and ear. The vestibule in the ear is part of the labyrinth, where it acts as a chamber between the semicircular canals and the cochlea. See *cochlea* and *labyrinth*.

Vibrio cholerae
The organism that causes cholera. The name *Vibrio* derives from the Latin because these curved rod-shaped bacteria possess a single polar flagellum and appear to vibrate when viewed under the microscope. *V. cholerae* was first isolated in pure culture in 1883 by Robert Koch, the discoverer of the tuberculosis organism, *Mycobacterium tuberculosis*. Cholera is usually a disease of poor sanitation. Humans are the only natural host for this organism and there have been six great pandemics (worldwide epidemics) of cholera. See *bacteria*.

Vice versa
'Conversely.'

Videlicet
'Namely' – normally this is abbreviated to 'viz'.

Vincat scientia morbos
'Let knowledge conquer disease.' Motto of the Royal Australasian College of Dental Surgeons.

Vincit qui se vincit
'First we must learn to overcome our own bad habits.' Literally he conquers who conquers himself.

Virgil (or Vergil)
Publius Vergilius Maro (70 BCE–19 BCE), a Latin poet, he wrote the *Eclogues*, the *Georgics*, and the *Aeneid*. The *Aeneid*, an epic poem of twelve books, was deservingly considered to be the Roman Empire's national epic.

Virgo intacta
'A maiden untouched' – Catullus. This reference is to the hymen membrane of the vagina, hence its presence was considered to be proof of virginity. See *Catullus* and *hymen*.

Virus
Disease producing microbes, incapable of independent life. They take over the DNA or RNA of a host's cells thereby making the host cells replicate countless versions of themselves. Originally, the word comes from the Latin *virus* and meant 'animal poison', be it from a scorpion, snake, etc. Pliny writes of the belief that wolves secreted a *virus amatorium* or love poison.

Viscera
Vital organs – plural of the Latin *viscus*, 'vital organ'. In anatomy we talk about the solid visceral organs, like the liver and kidneys, and the hollow visceral organs, like the stomach and bladder.

Vis medicatrix naturae

'The healing power of nature.' This is one of the basic principles of naturopathic medicine or naturopathy (nature cure). The aim is to maintain health by supporting and stimulating the *vis medicatrix naturae* – the healing power of nature. Rather than being a specific therapy, naturopathy is an holistic approach that stresses the importance of health maintenance, disease prevention as well as patient education.

Vita brevis, ars longa

'Life is short, art is long.' See *ars longa, vita brevis*.

Vita donum dei

'Life is the gift of god.' Motto of the Royal College of Midwives.

Vita enim mortuorum in memoria vivorum posita est

'The life of the dead retains a place in the memory of the living' – Cicero. See *Cicero*.

Vita si scias uti, longa est

'Life is long, if you know how to use it' – Seneca. See *Seneca*.

Viva voce

'Orally.' A viva voce generally means an oral examination, often the final step in a medical examination after taking written and clinical components.

Volvulus

A condition in which part of the intestine twists on itself – from *volvere*, 'to roll'. This is considered an acute surgical emergency that may well require surgery.

Vulgate

The Vulgate Bible was an early fifth-century translation of the Bible into Latin made by St Jerome on the orders of Pope Damasus I. It takes its name from the phrase *versio vulgata*, or 'the common version'. The Vulgate was designed to be both more accurate and easier to under- stand than its predecessors. It was the first – and for many centuries the only – Christian Bible translation that translated the Old Testament directly from the Hebrew original rather than indirectly from the Greek Septuagint.

Vulnera nisi sint tacta tractataque sanar non possunt

'Wounds cannot be cured unless handled and dressed' – Livy. See *Livy*.

Vulnus non penetrate animum

'A wound does not pierce the soul' – Macrobius. See *Macrobius*.

Vultus ac frons animi ianua

'The face and brow are the entrance of the mind' – Quintus Cicero. See *Quintus Cicero*.

Vulva

The female covering – from *vulva*, 'a covering'. The name given to the external female genitalia in front of the vaginal opening.

X

Xiphoid process
The tip of the breastbone. See *sternum*.

Z

Zygoma
The cheekbone – from the Greek, *zygoma*, 'the yoke'.

Zygomaticus major
The smiling muscle. This muscle is anchored on the zygoma or cheekbone and inserted into the upper fibres of the orbicularis oris muscle. When it contracts it pulls the mouth upwards into a smile.

Zygomaticus minor
The little smiling muscle, which helps its big brother, *zygomaticus major*.